Skillet
RECIPES

Publications International, Ltd.

Louis Weber, CEO
Publications International, Ltd.
8140 Lehigh Ave
Morton Grove, IL 60053

Pictured on the front cover: Shakshuka *(page 124).*

Pictured on the back cover *(clockwise from top left):* Balsamic Tomato Penne *(page 36),* Apple Berry Cinnamon Roll Cobbler *(page 186),* Red Cabbage with Bacon and Mushrooms *(page 158)* and BBQ Jackfruit *(page 60).*

ISBN: 978-1-63938-998-8

Manufactured in China.

8 7 6 5 4 3 2 1

Table of Contents

Sunrise & Shine Skillets

BLUEBERRY PANCAKES

- 2 tablespoons plus 2 teaspoons butter
- 1¼ cups milk
- 1 egg
- 1¼ cups all-purpose flour
- ¼ cup packed brown sugar
- 1 tablespoon baking powder
- ½ teaspoon salt
- ½ cup fresh blueberries, plus additional for serving
- Powdered sugar and/or maple syrup

1. Melt butter in large skillet or griddle over medium heat. Pour into medium bowl, leaving thin film of butter on skillet.
2. Whisk milk and egg into melted butter in bowl. Combine flour, brown sugar, baking powder and salt in large bowl; mix well. Add milk mixture; stir just until blended. *Do not overmix.* Gently stir in ½ cup blueberries.
3. Drop batter by ¼ cupfuls into skillet; cook over medium heat 2 to 3 minutes per side or until golden brown. Sprinkle pancakes with powdered sugar; serve with maple syrup and additional blueberries.

Makes 10 to 12 pancakes

ZUCCHINI-TOMATO FRITTATA

- 1 tablespoon olive oil
- 1 cup sliced zucchini
- 1 cup broccoli florets
- 1 cup diced red or yellow bell pepper
- 1 teaspoon salt, divided
- 6 eggs
- ½ cup cottage cheese
- ½ cup rehydrated* sun-dried tomatoes (1 ounce dry), coarsely chopped
- ¼ cup chopped green onions
- ¼ cup chopped fresh basil
- ⅛ teaspoon ground red pepper
- 2 tablespoons grated Parmesan cheese
- Paprika (optional)

**To rehydrate sun-dried tomatoes, pour 1 cup boiling water over tomatoes in small bowl; let stand 5 to 10 minutes or until softened. Drain well.*

1. Preheat broiler. Heat oil in large (10-inch) ovenproof skillet over medium-high heat. Add zucchini, broccoli and bell pepper and ½ teaspoon salt; cook and stir 3 to 4 minutes or until vegetables are crisp-tender.

2. Whisk eggs, cottage cheese, sun-dried tomatoes, green onions, basil, remaining ½ teaspoon salt and ground red pepper in medium bowl until well blended.

3. Pour egg mixture over vegetables in skillet. Cook over medium heat 7 to 8 minutes or until frittata is almost firm and golden brown on bottom, gently lifting sides of frittata so uncooked egg flows underneath. Remove from heat; sprinkle with cheese.

4. Broil about 5 inches from heat 3 to 4 minutes or until golden brown. Sprinkle with paprika, if desired. Cut into wedges.

Makes 4 servings

STRAWBERRY BANANA FRENCH TOAST

- 1 cup sliced fresh strawberries (about 8 medium)
- 2 teaspoons granulated sugar
- 2 eggs
- ½ cup milk
- 3 tablespoons all-purpose flour
- 1 teaspoon vanilla
- ⅛ teaspoon salt
- 1 tablespoon butter
- 4 slices (1 inch thick) egg bread or country bread
- 1 banana, cut into ¼-inch slices
- Whipped cream and powdered sugar (optional)
- Maple syrup

1. Combine strawberries and granulated sugar in small bowl; toss to coat. Set aside while preparing French toast.

2. Whisk eggs, milk, flour, vanilla and salt in shallow bowl or pie plate until well blended. Melt ½ tablespoon butter in large skillet over medium-high heat. Working with two slices at a time, dip bread into egg mixture, turning to coat completely; let excess drip off. Add to skillet; cook 3 to 4 minutes per side or until golden brown. Repeat with remaining butter and bread slices.

3. Top each serving with strawberry mixture and banana slices. Garnish with whipped cream and powdered sugar; serve with maple syrup.

Makes 2 servings

CHORIZO-POTATO HASH

- **1 pita or naan bread, torn into pieces**
- **5 tablespoons olive oil, divided**
- **Salt and black pepper**
- **1 pound uncooked Mexican chorizo sausage, casings removed**
- **1 onion, diced**
- **1 yellow bell pepper, diced**
- **1 red bell pepper, diced**
- **2 russet potatoes, peeled, grated, rinsed and squeezed dry *or* 1 package (20 ounces) refrigerated shredded hash brown potatoes**
- **1 green onion, diagonally sliced**

1. Place pita pieces in food processor; pulse until small crumbs form (about 15 pulses). Transfer to small bowl. Drizzle with 2 tablespoons oil; toss to coat.
2. Cook pita crumbs in large skillet over medium heat 6 to 8 minutes or until browned, stirring occasionally. Season with salt and black pepper. Remove to small bowl; set aside.
3. Add chorizo to skillet; cook over medium-high heat about 5 minutes or until browned, stirring to break up meat. Drain on paper towel-lined plate. Add onion and bell peppers to skillet; cook 8 minutes or until vegetables are tender, stirring occasionally. Season with salt and black pepper. Remove to medium bowl.
4. Add remaining 3 tablespoons oil to skillet. Spread potatoes in even layer; cook 3 minutes or until browned and beginning to crisp on bottom. Turn potatoes; cook 10 minutes or until tender and browned, stirring occasionally. Season with salt and black pepper. Stir in chorizo and vegetable mixture; cook 2 minutes or until heated through. Top with pita crumbs and green onion.

Makes 6 servings

DUTCH BABY PANCAKE

- 3 tablespoons butter, divided, plus additional for serving
- ½ cup all-purpose flour
- 2 tablespoons granulated sugar
- ¼ teaspoon salt
- ½ cup whole milk, at room temperature
- 2 eggs, at room temperature
- ¼ teaspoon vanilla
- Powdered sugar
- Lemon wedges

1. Preheat oven to 400°F. Place 1 tablespoon butter in large (9- to 10-inch) ovenproof skillet; place skillet in oven to heat while preparing batter. Melt remaining 2 tablespoons butter in small bowl; let cool slightly.
2. Combine flour, granulated sugar and salt in medium bowl; mix well. Add milk, eggs, melted butter and vanilla; whisk 1 minute or until batter is very smooth.
3. Remove skillet from oven; immediately pour batter into hot skillet.
4. Bake about 20 minutes or until outside of pancake is puffed and edges are deep golden brown. Sprinkle with powdered sugar; serve with lemon wedges and additional butter.

Makes 2 servings

CLASSIC BREAKFAST SANDWICH

2 English muffins, split
2 tablespoons butter, divided
2 slices American cheese
2 slices Canadian bacon
2 eggs
½ cup water

1. Toast English muffins; spread cut sides with 1 tablespoon butter. Place one slice cheese on bottom half of each muffin.
2. Melt ½ tablespoon butter in medium nonstick skillet over medium heat. Add Canadian bacon; cook about 2 minutes per side or until lightly browned. Remove to plate.
3. Spray insides of two round metal biscuit cutters (2⅞ to 3¼ inches) or quart-size canning rings with nonstick cooking spray. Melt remaining ½ tablespoon butter in same skillet over medium heat. Place rings in skillet; crack one egg into each ring and break yolk with fork. Pour water into skillet around rings; cover and cook 2 to 3 minutes or until eggs are set.
4. Gently remove eggs from rings. Place on cheese-topped muffin halves; top with Canadian bacon and remaining muffin halves. Wrap each sandwich in foil; let stand 2 minutes before serving. (Steam will melt cheese and blend flavors.)

Makes 2 servings

QUINOA BREAKFAST "FRIED RICE"

- 1 cup uncooked quinoa
- 1½ cups water
- ¼ teaspoon salt
- 2 tablespoons vegetable oil, divided
- 1 carrot, finely diced
- ¾ cup frozen peas
- 4 ounces deli ham, finely diced (optional)
- 2 green onions, thinly sliced
- 2 teaspoons minced garlic
- 1 teaspoon grated fresh ginger
- 3 eggs, lightly beaten
- ⅛ teaspoon salt
- 1 tablespoon reduced-sodium soy sauce, plus additional for serving
- 1 tablespoon ketchup
- ¼ teaspoon black pepper

1. Place quinoa in fine-mesh strainer; rinse well under cold water. Combine quinoa, 1½ cups water and salt in large saucepan; bring to a boil over medium-high heat. Reduce heat to low; cover and cook about 15 minutes or until quinoa is tender and water is absorbed. Spread on baking sheet; cool completely.

2. Heat 1 tablespoon oil in large nonstick skillet over medium-high heat. Add carrot and peas; cook and stir about 4 minutes or until softened. Add ham, if desired; cook about 2 minutes or until lightly browned. Add green onions, garlic and ginger; cook about 1 minute or until fragrant. Transfer to large bowl.

3. Heat remaining 1 tablespoon oil in skillet over medium-high heat. Add eggs and salt; cook about 1 minute or until lightly scrambled and set. Break up eggs into small, bite-size pieces with spatula.

4. Return vegetable mixture to skillet. Add quinoa; cook and stir 2 minutes. Add 1 tablespoon soy sauce, ketchup and pepper; cook and stir 1 minute or until heated through. Serve with additional soy sauce, if desired.

Makes 4 servings

CHOCOLATE CHIP PANCAKES

- **2 cups all-purpose flour**
- **2 teaspoons baking powder**
- **½ teaspoon baking soda**
- **½ teaspoon salt**
- **2 eggs**
- **2 cups plain yogurt**
- **¼ cup packed brown sugar**
- **¼ cup (½ stick) butter, melted**
- **1 cup mini chocolate chips**
- **Vegetable oil for cooking**
- **Powdered sugar and/or maple syrup**

1. Combine flour, baking powder, baking soda and salt in medium bowl; mix well. Beat eggs in another medium bowl. Whisk in yogurt, brown sugar and butter until well blended. Add to flour mixture; stir until almost blended. Add chocolate chips; stir just until flour mixture is moistened.

2. Heat 1 teaspoon oil in large nonstick skillet over medium heat. Drop batter by ¼ cupfuls into skillet; cook 3 minutes. Turn and cook 2 minutes or until browned on bottoms. Repeat with remaining batter, adding additional oil as needed. Sprinkle pancakes with powdered sugar; serve with maple syrup.

Makes 18 pancakes

Tip: To keep pancakes warm during cooking, preheat oven to 250°F. Place wire rack on large baking sheet and place in oven. Remove pancakes from skillet to wire rack after each batch.

BROCCOLI FRITTATA

- 1 broccoli crown
- 2 tablespoons olive oil
- 1 small red bell pepper, finely chopped
- 4 green onions, chopped
- 2 cloves garlic, minced
- 1 teaspoon smoked paprika
- ¾ teaspoon salt, divided
- 8 eggs
- ¼ cup milk
- ¼ cup grated Parmesan cheese
- ¼ teaspoon black pepper
- ¾ cup crumbled feta cheese

1. Preheat oven to 350°F. Peel off tough outer skin of broccoli stem with paring knife; chop stem into ¼-inch pieces. Cut top of broccoli into ½-inch florets.

2. Heat oil in large (10-inch) ovenproof nonstick skillet over medium-high heat. Add broccoli, cook 7 minutes, stirring occasionally. Add bell pepper, green onions, garlic, paprika and ¼ teaspoon salt; cook and stir 3 minutes or until bell pepper is softened.

3. Whisk eggs, milk, Parmesan, remaining ½ teaspoon salt and black pepper in medium bowl until well blended. Pour over vegetables in skillet; stir gently to make sure vegetables are spread out in skillet and egg mixture is evenly distributed. Cook about 2 minutes or until edges begin to set. Sprinkle with feta.

4. Transfer skillet to oven; bake about 20 minutes or just until eggs are set. Cool at least 5 minutes; cut into wedges. Serve warm or at room temperature.

Makes 6 servings

BREAKFAST BISCUIT BAKE

- **8 ounces bacon, chopped**
- **1 small onion, finely chopped**
- **1 clove garlic, minced**
- **¼ teaspoon red pepper flakes**
- **5 eggs**
- **¼ cup milk**
- **½ cup (2 ounces) shredded white Cheddar cheese, divided**
- **¼ teaspoon salt**
- **⅛ teaspoon black pepper**
- **1 package (16 ounces) refrigerated jumbo buttermilk biscuits (8 biscuits)**

1. Preheat oven to 425°F. Cook bacon in large ovenproof skillet until crisp. Remove to paper towel-lined plate. Drain off and reserve drippings, leaving 1 tablespoon in skillet.
2. Add onion, garlic and red pepper flakes to skillet; cook and stir over medium heat about 5 minutes or until onion is softened. Set aside to cool slightly.
3. Whisk eggs, milk, ¼ cup cheese, salt and black pepper in medium bowl until well blended. Stir in onion mixture.
4. Wipe out any onion mixture remaining in skillet with paper towel; grease with additional bacon drippings, if necessary. Separate biscuits and arrange in single layer in bottom of skillet. (Bottom of skillet should be completely covered.) Pour egg mixture over biscuits; sprinkle with remaining ¼ cup cheese and cooked bacon.
5. Bake 25 minutes or until puffed and golden brown. Serve warm.

Makes 8 servings

FRENCH ONION PASTA

¼ cup (½ stick) butter
1½ pounds yellow onions (3 medium), thinly sliced
¾ teaspoon salt, divided
¼ teaspoon black pepper
2 tablespoons olive oil
2 cups cubed French or Italian bread
⅓ cup sherry or white wine
12 ounces uncooked campanelle or other short pasta shape
4 cups mushroom or vegetable broth
6 fresh thyme sprigs
¼ cup whipping cream
1½ cups (6 ounces) shredded Gruyère or Swiss cheese

1. Melt butter in large skillet over medium-low heat. Add onions; cook about 45 minutes or until onions are dark golden brown, stirring frequently and adding water by tablespoons if onions are too dry. Stir in ¼ teaspoon salt and black pepper.

2. Meanwhile, preheat oven to 350°F. Combine bread cubes and oil in large bowl; toss to coat. Spread on baking sheet; bake 20 minutes or until bread cubes are toasted, stirring once.

3. Add sherry to onions in skillet; cook over medium-high heat, scraping up browned bits from bottom of skillet. Add pasta, broth, thyme sprigs and remaining ½ teaspoon salt; mix well. Bring to a boil; cook 10 minutes or until broth is absorbed and pasta is tender, stirring frequently.

4. Remove from heat; remove thyme springs. Top with cheese; cover and let stand until cheese is melted, or broil until cheese is melted and browned. Top with toasted bread cubes.

Makes 4 to 6 servings

ASIAN CHICKEN AND NOODLE STIR-FRY

- 8 ounces uncooked thin Pad Thai rice noodles (⅛-inch wide)
- 1 tablespoon vegetable oil
- 1 pound boneless skinless chicken breasts, cut into 1×½-inch pieces
- 2 cloves garlic, minced
- 1 bottle (12 ounces) stir-fry sauce
- ¼ cup water
- 2 tablespoons packed brown sugar
- 1 package (16 ounces) frozen stir-fry vegetable blend (do not thaw)

1. Cook or soak noodles according to package directions until almost tender.
2. Heat oil in large skillet over high heat. Add chicken; cook and stir 4 minutes or until no longer pink. Add garlic; cook and stir 30 seconds. Remove chicken to plate.
3. Add stir-fry sauce, water and brown sugar to skillet, scraping up browned bits from bottom of skillet. Stir in noodles, vegetables and chicken; cook until vegetables are tender and noodles are saucy.

Makes 4 servings

MINESTRONE SKILLET DINNER

- 2 slices bacon, coarsely chopped
- 1 tablespoon olive oil
- 2 cups coarsely shredded or chopped cabbage
- 1 zucchini, cut into ½-inch pieces
- 1 onion, chopped
- ¾ cup chopped carrots
- 1 stalk celery, chopped
- 1 clove garlic, minced
- 1 can (about 14 ounces) diced tomatoes
- 1 cup cooked macaroni
- ¾ cup canned Great Northern beans, rinsed and drained
- 1 teaspoon salt
- ½ teaspoon dried oregano
- ¼ teaspoon dried thyme
- ⅔ cup shredded Parmesan cheese

1. Preheat oven to 350°F. Cook bacon in large ovenproof skillet over medium heat 5 minutes or until crisp-tender. Drain on paper towel-lined plate.
2. Heat oil in same skillet over medium-high heat. Add cabbage, zucchini, onion, carrots, celery and garlic; cook 10 minutes or until cabbage is crisp-tender, stirring frequently.
3. Stir in tomatoes, macaroni, beans, bacon, salt, oregano and thyme; cook over medium heat 5 minutes. Sprinkle with cheese.
4. Bake 15 minutes or until hot and bubbly.

Makes 4 servings

Tip: For a vegetarian dish, omit the bacon and increase the olive oil to 2 tablespoons.

SKILLET MAC AND CHEESE

- 1 pound uncooked cavatappi or rotini pasta
- 8 ounces thick-cut bacon, cut into ½-inch pieces
- ¼ cup finely chopped onion
- ¼ cup all-purpose flour
- 3½ cups whole milk
- 1 cup (4 ounces) shredded white Cheddar cheese
- 1 cup (4 ounces) shredded fontina cheese
- 1 cup (4 ounces) shredded Gruyère cheese
- ¾ cup grated Parmesan cheese, divided
- ½ teaspoon salt
- ½ teaspoon dry mustard
- ¼ teaspoon ground red pepper
- ¼ teaspoon black pepper
- ¼ cup panko bread crumbs

1. Preheat oven to 400°F. Cook pasta according to package directions for al dente; drain.
2. Meanwhile, cook bacon in large ovenproof skillet until crisp; drain on paper towel-lined plate. Pour drippings into glass measuring cup, leaving thin coating on skillet.
3. Heat 4 tablespoons drippings in large saucepan over medium-high heat. Add onion; cook and stir 4 minutes or until translucent. Add flour; cook and stir 5 minutes. Slowly add milk over medium-low heat, stirring constantly. Stir in Cheddar, fontina, Gruyère, ½ cup Parmesan, salt, mustard, red pepper and black pepper until smooth and well blended. Add cooked pasta; stir gently to coat. Stir in bacon.
4. Spoon pasta mixture into skillet; spread in even layer. Combine panko and remaining ¼ cup Parmesan in small bowl; sprinkle over pasta.
5. Bake 30 minutes or until top is golden brown.

Makes 6 servings

SZECHUAN BEEF LO MEIN

- 1 boneless beef top sirloin steak (about 1 pound)
- 4 cloves garlic, minced
- 2 teaspoons minced fresh ginger
- ¾ teaspoon red pepper flakes, divided
- 1 tablespoon vegetable oil
- 1 can (about 14 ounces) vegetable broth
- 1 cup water
- 2 tablespoons soy sauce
- 1 package (8 ounces) frozen mixed vegetables for stir-fry
- 1 package (9 ounces) refrigerated angel hair pasta
- ¼ cup chopped fresh cilantro (optional)

1. Cut beef in half lengthwise, then cut crosswise into thin slices. Combine beef, garlic, ginger and ½ teaspoon red pepper flakes in medium bowl; toss to coat.
2. Heat oil in large skillet over medium-high heat. Add half of beef; cook and stir 2 minutes or until beef is barely pink in center. Remove to plate; repeat with remaining beef.
3. Add broth, water, soy sauce and remaining ¼ teaspoon red pepper flakes to skillet; bring to a boil over high heat. Add vegetables; return to a boil. Reduce heat to low; cover and simmer 3 minutes or until vegetables are crisp-tender.
4. Stir in pasta; return to a boil over high heat. Reduce heat to medium; simmer, uncovered, 2 minutes, separating pasta with two forks. Return beef to skillet; cook 1 minute or until pasta is tender and beef is heated through. Sprinkle with cilantro, if desired.

Makes 4 servings

BALSAMIC TOMATO PENNE

- 1 package (16 ounces) uncooked penne pasta
- 6 tablespoons olive oil, divided
- ½ red onion, cut into ⅛-inch slices (1 cup)
- ¼ cup balsamic vinegar
- 4 plum tomatoes, cut into ½-inch pieces (2½ cups)
- 6 cloves roasted garlic*
- 1 teaspoon salt
- 1 package (5 ounces) fresh spinach, stemmed
- Shredded Parmesan cheese

**To roast garlic, cut top off one head of garlic to expose top of cloves. Place on piece of foil; drizzle with 1 teaspoon olive oil and season lightly with salt. Wrap tightly in foil. Roast at 400°F 35 to 40 minutes or until soft. Squeeze garlic from skins when cool enough to handle.*

1. Cook pasta according to package directions for al dente. Drain and place in large serving bowl; stir in 2 tablespoons oil.
2. Meanwhile, heat remaining ¼ cup oil in large skillet over medium-high heat. Add onion; cook and stir 5 minutes or until softened. Reduce heat to medium. Add vinegar; cook 3 minutes or until slightly reduced.
3. Add tomatoes, roasted garlic and salt; cook and stir 1 minute. Add spinach; cook 1 minute or just until wilted. Pour sauce over pasta; stir to coat. Serve with cheese.

Makes 4 to 6 servings

ALFREDO BOLOGNESE SPAGHETTI SKILLET

- 1 package (16 ounces) uncooked spaghetti
- 1 jar (about 15 ounces) alfredo sauce
- 1 pound ground beef or ground meat substitute
- 1 onion, chopped
- 2 cloves garlic, minced
- 1 teaspoon Italian seasoning
- ½ teaspoon salt
- ¼ teaspoon black pepper
- 1 jar (about 24 ounces) marinara sauce
- 1 cup (4 ounces) shredded mozzarella cheese
- Red pepper flakes (optional)

1. Preheat oven to 350°F. Cook pasta according to package directions for al dente. Drain and return to saucepan; stir in alfredo sauce. Cover and keep warm.
2. Meanwhile, cook beef, onion and garlic in large ovenproof skillet over medium-high heat 6 to 8 minutes or until beef is no longer pink, stirring to break up meat. Stir in Italian seasoning, salt and black pepper. Reduce heat to medium-low; add marinara sauce and cook 10 minutes, stirring frequently.
3. Transfer sauce to large bowl. Spread spaghetti mixture in skillet; top with meat sauce and sprinkle with cheese.
4. Bake 20 minutes or until pasta is heated through and cheese is melted. Sprinkle with red pepper flakes, if desired.

Makes 6 to 8 servings

MUSHROOM NOODLE STIR-FRY

- 8 ounces uncooked Chinese egg noodles or spaghetti
- 8 ounces shiitake mushrooms, stemmed and thinly sliced (¼-inch slices)
- Pinch of salt
- 2 tablespoons butter
- 1 tablespoon minced garlic
- 2 teaspoons honey
- ½ cup stir-fry sauce
- 2 to 3 tablespoons water
- 2 green onions, sliced diagonally
- 2 tablespoons grated Parmesan cheese

1. Cook noodles according to package directions; drain and rinse under cold water to stop cooking.
2. Heat large skillet over medium-high heat. Add mushrooms; cook and stir about 5 minutes or until browned. Season with salt. Add butter, garlic and honey; cook and stir 1 minute or until butter is melted and garlic is fragrant but not browned.
3. Add stir-fry sauce, 2 tablespoons water and noodles; cook and stir 2 to 3 minutes or until heated through. Add additional water by teaspoonful, if necessary, to loosen sauce. Divide noodles between serving bowls; top with green onions and cheese.

Makes 2 main-dish or 4 side-dish servings

SKILLET VEGETABLE LASAGNA

- 8 ounces hot Italian sausage, casings removed
- 8 ounces ground beef
- 2 stalks celery, sliced
- ⅓ cup chopped onion
- 2 cups marinara sauce
- 1⅓ cups water
- ¾ teaspoon salt
- 4 ounces uncooked bowtie (farfalle) pasta
- 1 medium zucchini, halved lengthwise, then cut crosswise into ½-inch slices (2 cups)
- ¾ cup chopped green or yellow bell pepper
- ½ cup (2 ounces) shredded mozzarella cheese
- ½ cup ricotta cheese
- 2 tablespoons finely grated Parmesan cheese

1. Combine sausage, beef, celery and onion in large skillet; cook over medium-high heat 6 to 8 minutes or until beef is no longer pink, stirring to break up meat.
2. Stir in marinara sauce, water and salt; bring to a boil. Stir in pasta. Reduce heat to medium-low; cover and cook 12 minutes.
3. Stir in zucchini and bell pepper; cover and cook 2 minutes. Uncover; cook 4 to 6 minutes or until vegetables are crisp-tender.
4. Sprinkle with mozzarella. Combine ricotta and Parmesan in small bowl; mix well. Drop by rounded teaspoonfuls on top of pasta mixture in skillet. Remove from heat; cover and let stand 10 minutes before serving.

Makes 4 servings

RICE NOODLES WITH BROCCOLI AND TOFU

- 1 package (14 ounces) firm or extra firm tofu
- 1 package (8 to 10 ounces) wide rice noodles
- 2 tablespoons peanut oil
- 3 medium shallots, sliced
- 6 cloves garlic, minced
- 1 jalapeño pepper, minced
- 2 teaspoons minced fresh ginger
- 3 cups broccoli florets
- ¼ cup soy sauce
- 1 to 2 tablespoons fish sauce*
- Fresh basil leaves (optional)

**To make this dish vegetarian, look for vegetarian fish sauce or substitute additional soy sauce or fresh lime juice.*

1. Drain tofu and press between paper towels to remove excess water. Cut tofu into bite-size pieces.
2. Meanwhile, place noodles in medium bowl. Cover with hot water; let stand 15 minutes or until tender. Drain.
3. Heat oil in large skillet over medium-high heat. Add tofu; cook and stir 5 minutes or until tofu is lightly browned on all sides. Remove to plate.
4. Add shallots, garlic, jalapeño and ginger to skillet; cook and stir 2 to 3 minutes. Add broccoli; cook and stir 1 minute. Cover and cook 3 minutes or until broccoli is crisp-tender.
5. Add tofu, noodles, soy sauce and fish sauce to skillet; cook 8 minutes or until heated through, stirring frequently. Garnish with basil.

Makes 4 servings

GREEK CHICKEN AND PASTA

- **8 ounces uncooked fettuccine**
- **1 jar (6 ounces) marinated artichoke hearts**
- **1 tablespoon olive oil, divided**
- **1 small red bell pepper, cut into thin strips**
- **3 cloves garlic, minced**
- **1 pound boneless skinless chicken breasts, cut into bite-size pieces**
- **1 tablespoon plus 1 teaspoon lemon juice**
- **1½ teaspoons dried oregano**
- **1 teaspoon grated lemon peel**
- **¼ to ½ teaspoon dried mint (optional)**
- **¼ teaspoon black pepper**
- **⅓ cup sliced pitted black olives**
- **¼ cup (1 ounce) crumbled feta cheese**

1. Cook fettuccine according to package directions for al dente; drain and keep warm.
2. Drain artichokes, reserving marinade. Cut artichokes into quarters.
3. Heat ½ tablespoon oil in large skillet over medium heat. Add bell pepper and garlic; cook and stir about 3 minutes or until tender. Remove to plate.
4. Add chicken and remaining ½ tablespoon oil to skillet; cook and stir 2 to 3 minutes or until chicken is almost cooked through.
5. Return bell pepper to skillet with reserved artichoke marinade, lemon juice, oregano, lemon peel, mint, if desired, and black pepper; bring to a boil. Reduce heat to low; cook 1 to 2 minutes or until chicken is no longer pink. Stir in artichokes and olives; cook 2 minutes or until heated through. Add pasta; stir gently to coat. Sprinkle with cheese.

Makes 4 servings

CREAMY SPINACH SKILLET GNOCCHI

- 2 tablespoons butter
- 2 tablespoons olive oil, divided
- 1 package (about 17 ounces) shelf-stable gnocchi
- 3 cloves garlic, minced
- 1 can (about 14 ounces) diced tomatoes
- ½ teaspoon salt
- ½ teaspoon Italian seasoning
- ¼ teaspoon black pepper
- 1 package (8 to 10 ounces) fresh spinach, stemmed and torn
- ¼ cup whipping cream
- ¼ cup grated Parmesan cheese, plus additional for garnish
- Chopped fresh basil (optional)

1. Heat butter and 1 tablespoon oil in large skillet over medium-high heat. Add gnocchi; cook about 5 minutes or until golden brown, stirring occasionally. Transfer gnocchi to medium bowl.

2. Add remaining 1 tablespoon oil to skillet; heat over medium-high heat. Add garlic; cook and stir 10 seconds or until sizzling. Carefully add tomatoes (they will splatter); cook and stir until tomatoes are saucy and juice is thickened. Stir in salt, Italian seasoning and pepper. Stir in spinach by handfuls, stirring until wilted after each addition.

3. Return gnocchi to skillet; stir in cream and ¼ cup cheese. Cook and stir until well blended. Sprinkle with basil, if desired. Serve immediately.

Makes 4 to 6 servings

Sandwiches & Wraps

GRILLED PB AND J SANDWICHES

- 2 tablespoons creamy or chunky peanut butter
- 4 slices cinnamon raisin or whole wheat bread
- 2 tablespoons grape or strawberry jelly
- 1 tablespoon butter, softened

1. Spread peanut butter evenly over two bread slices; top with jelly and remaining bread slices.
2. Spread butter on outside of each sandwich.
3. Cook sandwiches in large nonstick skillet over medium heat about 2 minutes per side or until golden brown.

Makes 2 servings

Variations: Add a layer of thinly sliced banana or apple between the peanut butter and jelly. Swap out the peanut butter for almond butter or cashew butter. Or cook the sandwiches French toast-style, dipping them in an egg-milk mixture (see page 8) and cooking in butter until golden brown.

SHREDDED BEEF TACOS

- 1 tablespoon vegetable oil
- 1 pound boneless beef chuck, cut into 1-inch cubes
- 2 teaspoons chili powder
- 1 clove garlic, minced
- ½ teaspoon salt
- ½ teaspoon ground cumin
- 1 can (about 14 ounces) diced tomatoes
- 12 (6-inch) hard taco shells
- 1 cup (4 ounces) shredded Cheddar cheese
- 1 to 2 cups shredded iceberg lettuce
- 1 large tomato, seeded and chopped

1. Heat oil in large skillet over medium-high heat. Add beef; cook 10 to 12 minutes or until browned on all sides, stirring occasionally.
2. Add chili powder, garlic, salt and cumin; cook and stir 30 seconds. Add diced tomatoes; bring to a boil. Reduce heat to low; cover and simmer 1½ to 2 hours or until beef is very tender.
3. Pull beef into coarse shreds in skillet using two forks. Increase heat to medium; cook, uncovered, 10 to 15 minutes or until most of liquid has evaporated.
4. Fill taco shells with beef, cheese, lettuce and chopped tomato.

Makes 6 servings

TURKEY POBLANO BURRITOS

- 1 tablespoon vegetable oil
- 2 medium poblano peppers, seeded and chopped
- ½ cup chopped onion
- 2 cans (about 10 ounces each) diced tomatoes with green chilies
- 3 cups cooked rice
- 2 cups chopped cooked turkey or chicken
- 1 can (about 15 ounces) black beans, rinsed and drained
- 1½ cups (6 ounces) shredded Cheddar cheese or Mexican cheese blend, divided
- ½ cup sour cream
- 8 (10-inch) flour tortillas
- ¼ cup chopped fresh cilantro

1. Heat oil in large skillet over medium heat. Add poblanos and onion; cook 8 minutes or until vegetables are tender, stirring occasionally.
2. Stir in tomatoes, rice, turkey and beans; bring to a boil. Reduce heat to low; simmer 10 minutes. Remove from heat. Top with 1 cup cheese; cover and let stand 5 minutes or until cheese is melted.
3. Spread 1 tablespoon sour cream over each tortilla. Spoon rice mixture down centers of tortillas; top with remaining ½ cup cheese and sprinkle with cilantro. Roll up tortillas to enclose filling.

Makes 8 servings

CRISPY ONION FRITTATA SANDWICH

- 8 eggs
- 1 cup French fried onions, divided
- 1 cup (4 ounces) shredded Monterey Jack, white Cheddar or Swiss cheese, divided
- ¼ cup water
- 2 tablespoons chopped fresh Italian parsley
- ½ teaspoon salt
- ⅛ teaspoon black pepper
- 1 tablespoon butter
- 1 round loaf (7 to 8 inches) sourdough or Italian bread
- ¼ cup garlic mayonnaise
- 1½ cups mixed greens or baby arugula
- 1 cup thinly sliced roasted red peppers

1. Whisk eggs, ⅓ cup onions, ⅓ cup cheese, water, parsley, salt and pepper in medium bowl until well blended.
2. Melt butter in medium (8- to 9-inch) nonstick skillet over medium heat. Add egg mixture; cook without stirring 2 minutes or until edge begins to set. Use spatula to gently stir and lift cooked portions to allow uncooked egg to flow underneath. Cook about 5 minutes or until eggs are set on bottom and almost set on top.
3. Sprinkle with remaining ⅔ cup cheese; cover and cook 2 minutes or until cheese is melted and top of frittata is set.
4. Cut bread in half crosswise; remove excess bread from inside of loaf, if desired. Spread mayonnaise over cut sides of bread. Slide frittata onto bottom half of bread; top with remaining ⅔ cup onions, mixed greens, roasted peppers and top half of bread. Cut into wedges.

Makes 4 to 6 servings

BEEF AND BEAN BURRITOS

- 8 ounces ground beef
- ½ cup chopped onion
- ½ cup chopped red or green bell pepper
- 2 teaspoons chili powder
- 1 can (about 15 ounces) black beans, rinsed and drained
- ½ to ¾ cup salsa verde
- 4 (8-inch) flour tortillas
- ½ cup shredded Mexican cheese
- ¼ to ½ cup chopped fresh cilantro

1. Cook beef, onion and bell pepper in large skillet over medium-high heat about 5 minutes or until beef is no longer pink, stirring to break up meat. Drain fat.
2. Add chili powder; cook and stir 1 minute. Stir in beans and salsa verde; cook 3 to 4 minutes or until heated through.
3. Heat tortillas according to package directions. Spoon meat mixture down centers of tortillas; top with cheese and cilantro. Roll up tortillas to enclose filling.

Makes 4 servings

BBQ JACKFRUIT

- 1½ cups ketchup
- ⅓ cup packed brown sugar
- ¼ cup cider vinegar
- 2 tablespoons molasses
- 1 tablespoon dry mustard
- 2 cloves garlic, minced
- 2 teaspoons onion powder
- 2 teaspoons chili powder
- 1 teaspoon paprika
- 1 teaspoons ground cumin
- ⅛ teaspoon ground red pepper
- 2 cans (20 ounces each) young jackfruit in water or brine
- 1 tablespoon olive oil
- 1 onion, chopped
- ½ cup water
- Coleslaw or shredded cabbage
- 6 to 8 hamburger buns

1. For sauce, combine ketchup, brown sugar, vinegar, molasses, dry mustard, garlic, onion powder, chili powder, paprika, cumin and red pepper in medium saucepan; bring to a boil over medium- high heat. Reduce heat to medium-low; coverand simmer 20 minutes or until slightly thickened, stirring occasionally.
2. Meanwhile, drain jackfruit and rinse well. Cut off and discard tough core parts; shred remaining jackfruit with fingers.
3. Heat oil in large skillet over medium-high heat. Add onion; cook and stir 8 to 10 minutes or until lightly browned. Add jackfruit; cook and stir 5 minutes. Stir in 1 cup barbecue sauce and water. Reduce heat to medium-low; cover and simmer 20 minutes. Uncover; cook and stir until thickened, adding additional barbecue sauce, if desired.
4. Serve jackfruit and coleslaw on buns with additional sauce.

Makes 6 to 8 servings

MU SHU PORK WRAPS

- 1 tablespoon dark sesame oil
- 1 red bell pepper, cut into short, thin strips
- 1 small pork tenderloin (about 12 ounces), cut into strips
- 1 medium zucchini or summer squash (or a combination), cut into strips
- 3 cloves garlic, minced
- 2 cups prepared coleslaw mix or shredded cabbage
- 2 tablespoons hoisin sauce
- 4 (10-inch) sandwich wraps or flour tortillas
- ¼ cup plum sauce

1. Heat oil in large skillet over medium-high heat. Add bell pepper; cook and stir 2 minutes. Add pork, zucchini and garlic; cook and stir 4 to 5 minutes or until pork is cooked through and vegetables are crisp-tender.
2. Add coleslaw mix; cook and stir 2 minutes or until wilted. Add hoisin sauce; cook and stir 1 minute.
3. Heat wraps according to package directions. Spread plum sauce down centers of wraps; top with pork mixture. Roll up to enclose filling; cut diagonally in half.

Makes 4 servings

CALIFORNIA BBQ BURGERS

- **4 tablespoons barbecue sauce, divided**
- **2 tablespoons mayonnaise**
- **1 medium onion, divided**
- **1 pound ground beef**
- **1 teaspoon olive oil**
- **½ teaspoon salt**
- **¼ teaspoon black pepper**
- **4 burger buns, split and toasted**
- **1 ripe avocado, sliced**

1. Combine 2 tablespoons barbecue sauce and mayonnaise in small bowl; set aside. Cut ½ inch off top of onion; finely chop. (You should have about 1½ tablespoons.) Cut remaining onion into ¼-inch slices.
2. Combine beef, chopped onion and 1 tablespoon barbecue sauce in medium bowl; mix gently. Shape into four patties (about ½ inch thick); press indentation into center of each patty with thumb or fingertips.
3. Heat oil in large skillet (preferably cast iron) over medium-high heat. Add sliced onion; cook 5 minutes or until onion is softened and beginning to brown, stirring occasionally. Remove to small bowl; stir in remaining 1 tablespoon barbecue sauce. Wipe out skillet with paper towel.
4. Return skillet to medium-high heat; heat 2 to 3 minutes or until very hot. Season both sides of patties with salt and pepper; add patties to skillet. Cook 4 minutes; turn and cook about 3 minutes for medium (145°F) or until desired doneness.
5. Spread 1 tablespoon mayonnaise mixture on top half of each bun. Place burgers on bottom halves of buns; top with cooked onions, avocado and top halves of buns.

Makes 4 servings

CHORIZO AND PAPA BURRITOS

- 14 ounces uncooked Mexican chorizo sausage
- 2 small russet potatoes, peeled and diced (about 6 ounces)
- 8 taco-size flour tortillas
- ½ cup (2 ounces) shredded Monterey Jack cheese
- ¼ cup sour cream

1. Remove and discard casing from chorizo. Crumble chorizo into large skillet; cook over medium-high heat 6 to 8 minutes or until browned, stirring to break up meat.
2. When chorizo begins to release fat, add potatoes to skillet. Cook about 12 minutes or until potatoes are tender, stirring frequently. Drain excess fat.
3. Heat tortillas: On a gas stove, place tortilla directly on burner over low flame; turn with tongs when tortilla begins to brown, about 10 seconds. Heat until browned on both sides. On an electric range, preheat burner 2 minutes on medium heat. Place tortilla directly onto burner; turn with tongs when tortilla begins to brown, about 10 seconds. Heat until browned on both sides.
4. Spoon about ¼ cup chorizo mixture down center of each tortilla; top with 1 tablespoon cheese and 1½ teaspoons sour cream. Roll up tortillas to enclose filling.

Makes 8 mini burritos

Tip: For larger burritos, use four fajita-size flour tortillas and ½ cup filling per tortilla.

MUSHROOM CHEESESTEAK SANDWICHES

- **8 ounces mushrooms, cut into ½-inch slices**
- **1½ teaspoons salt, divided**
- **2 tablespoons vegetable oil, divided**
- **1 medium onion, cut into ½-inch slices**
- **1 green bell pepper, cut into ½-inch slices**
- **½ teaspoon garlic powder**
- **½ teaspoon black pepper, divided**
- **1 pound skirt or flank steak**
- **4 French bread or hoagie rolls, split and toasted**
- **8 slices provolone cheese**

1. Place mushrooms in large dry skillet;* add ¾ teaspoon salt and cook over medium-high heat about 5 minutes or until mushrooms release their liquid and begin to brown, stirring occasionally. Add 1 tablespoon oil, onion, bell pepper, garlic powder and ¼ teaspoon black pepper to skillet; cook 6 to 8 minutes or until onion and bell pepper begin to brown, stirring occasionally.

2. While vegetables are cooking, cut steak in half lengthwise, then cut crosswise (against the grain) into ¼-inch slices. Season with remaining ¾ teaspoon salt and ¼ teaspoon black pepper.

3. Remove vegetables to medium bowl; cover to keep warm. Heat remaining 1 tablespoon oil in same skillet over medium-high heat. Add steak in single layer; cook 1 to 2 minutes per side or just until edges are browned. Add steak and any juices in skillet to vegetables in bowl; stir to blend.

4. Spoon one fourth of steak and vegetable mixture on bottom half of each roll; top with two slices cheese and top half of roll. If desired, cover sandwiches loosely with foil and let stand briefly to melt cheese, or place sandwiches in 300°F oven to melt cheese.

**For better browning of steak and vegetables, do not use a nonstick skillet.*

Makes 4 servings

Hearty Grains & Beans

BLACK BEANS WITH BACON AND POBLANO PEPPERS

- 2 slices bacon
- 2 medium poblano peppers, chopped (about 1 cup)
- 1 small onion, chopped
- 2 cloves garlic, minced
- 1 teaspoon salt, divided
- ½ teaspoon chili powder
- 1 can (about 15 ounces) black beans, rinsed and drained
- ⅓ cup water

1. Cook bacon in large skillet over medium heat 6 to 7 minutes or until crisp, turning occasionally. Drain on paper towel-lined plate. Chop bacon; set aside.
2. Add poblanos, onion, garlic, ½ teaspoon salt and chili powder to same skillet; cook and stir 5 minutes or until vegetables are crisp-tender. Add beans, water and remaining ½ teaspoon salt; cook 10 minutes or until liquid is absorbed and vegetables are tender, stirring occasionally.
3. Stir in bacon just before serving.

Makes 4 servings

SPANISH BRAISED CHICKEN WITH GREEN OLIVES AND RICE

- 2 pounds bone-in chicken thighs, skin removed
- 1 teaspoon paprika
- ½ teaspoon salt, divided
- 2 tablespoons olive oil
- ¾ cup dry sherry
- 2¼ cups water
- 1 can (about 14 ounces) chicken broth
- ¾ cup pimiento-stuffed green olives
- 1½ teaspoons dried sage
- 1½ cups uncooked long grain white rice

1. Sprinkle chicken with paprika and ¼ teaspoon salt. Heat oil in large skillet over medium-high heat. Add chicken; cook 3 to 4 minutes per side or until browned. Remove to plate.

2. Add sherry to skillet, scraping up browned bits from bottom of skillet. Stir in water, broth, olives, sage and remaining ¼ teaspoon salt; bring to a boil. Reduce heat to low. Return chicken to skillet; cover and simmer 10 minutes.

3. Add rice to liquid around chicken; stir gently to distribute rice evenly in skillet. Cover and simmer 20 to 25 minutes or until rice is tender and chicken is cooked through (165°F).

Makes 6 servings

CHICKEN SAUSAGE AND TWO-GRAIN SKILLET

- 1 tablespoon olive oil
- 1 package (12 ounces) fully cooked chicken apple sausage links, sliced
- 1 can (about 14 ounces) chicken broth
- 1 cup uncooked instant brown rice
- ½ cup uncooked quinoa
- 1 red bell pepper, cut into thin strips
- 1 stalk celery, cut diagonally into ¼-inch slices
- 1½ teaspoons curry powder *or* 1 teaspoon ground turmeric
- ½ cup thawed frozen peas
- Salt and black pepper
- ¼ cup chopped green onions (optional)

1. Heat oil in large skillet over medium-high heat. Add sausage; cook 3 minutes or until edges are browned, stirring occasionally.
2. Stir in broth, rice, quinoa, bell pepper, celery and curry powder; bring to a boil. Reduce heat to low; cover and simmer 12 minutes or until liquid is absorbed.
3. Remove from heat. Stir in peas; let stand 5 minutes. Season with salt and black pepper; sprinkle with green onions, if desired.

Makes 4 servings

BROWN RICE WITH CHICKPEAS, SPINACH AND FETA

- 1 tablespoon olive oil
- ½ cup diced celery
- 2 cups water
- 1 can (about 15 ounces) chickpeas, rinsed and drained
- 1 package (10 ounces) frozen chopped spinach, thawed and squeezed dry
- ½ cup uncooked instant brown rice
- 1 teaspoon Greek or Italian seasoning
- 1 clove garlic, minced
- ¼ teaspoon salt
- ⅛ teaspoon black pepper
- ½ cup (2 ounces) crumbled feta cheese
- 1 tablespoon lemon juice

1. Heat oil in large skillet over medium-high heat. Add celery; cook about 4 minutes or until lightly browned in spots, stirring occasionally.
2. Stir in water, chickpeas, spinach, rice, Greek seasoning, garlic, salt and pepper; bring to a boil. Reduce heat to low; cover and simmer 12 minutes or until rice is tender.
3. Remove from heat; stir in cheese and lemon juice.

Makes 4 servings

SAUSAGE AND BEAN STEW

- 2 cups fresh bread crumbs*
- 2 tablespoons olive oil, divided
- 1 pound uncooked pork sausage, cut into 2-inch pieces
- 1 leek, cut in half lengthwise and thinly sliced
- 1 large onion, cut into quarters and cut into ¼-inch slices
- 1 teaspoon salt, divided
- 2 cloves garlic, minced
- ½ teaspoon dried thyme
- ½ teaspoon ground sage
- ¼ teaspoon paprika
- ¼ teaspoon ground allspice
- ¼ teaspoon black pepper
- 1 can (28 ounces) diced tomatoes
- 2 cans (about 15 ounces each) navy or cannellini beans, rinsed and drained
- 2 tablespoons whole grain mustard
- Fresh thyme leaves (optional)

**To make bread crumbs, cut 4 ounces stale baguette or country bread into several pieces; pulse in food processor until coarse crumbs form.*

1. Preheat oven to 350°F. Combine bread crumbs and 1 tablespoon oil in medium bowl; mix well.
2. Heat remaining 1 tablespoon oil in large ovenproof skillet over medium-high heat. Add sausage; cook 8 minutes or until browned, stirring occasionally. (Sausage will not be cooked through.) Remove to plate.
3. Add leek, onion and ½ teaspoon salt to skillet; cook 10 minutes or until vegetables are soft and beginning to brown, stirring occasionally. Add garlic; cook and stir 1 minute. Add dried thyme, sage, paprika, allspice and pepper; cook and stir 1 minute. Add tomatoes; cook 5 minutes, stirring occasionally. Stir in beans, mustard and remaining ½ teaspoon salt; bring to a simmer.
4. Return sausage to skillet, pushing down into bean mixture. Sprinkle with bread crumbs.
5. Bake 25 minutes or until bread crumbs are lightly browned and sausage is cooked through. Garnish with fresh thyme.

Makes 4 to 6 servings

CHICKEN FRIED RICE

- 2 tablespoons vegetable oil, divided
- 12 ounces boneless skinless chicken breasts, cut into ½-inch cubes
- Salt and black pepper
- 2 tablespoons butter
- 2 cloves garlic, minced
- ½ sweet onion, diced
- 1 medium carrot, diced
- 2 green onions, thinly sliced, plus additional for garnish
- 3 eggs
- 4 cups cooked rice*
- 3 tablespoons soy sauce
- 2 tablespoons sesame seeds

**For rice, cook 1½ cups rice according to package directions without oil or butter. Spread hot rice on large rimmed baking sheet; cool to room temperature. Refrigerate several hours or overnight. Measure 4 cups for recipe.*

1. Heat 1 tablespoon oil in large skillet over medium-high heat. Add chicken; season with salt and pepper. Cook and stir 5 to 6 minutes or until cooked through. Add butter and garlic; cook and stir 1 minute or until butter is melted. Remove to medium bowl.

2. Add sweet onion, carrot and two green onions to skillet; cook and stir over high heat 3 minutes or until vegetables are softened. Add to bowl with chicken.

3. Heat remaining 1 tablespoon oil in same skillet. Crack eggs into skillet; cook and stir 45 seconds or until eggs are scrambled but still moist. Return chicken and vegetable mixture to skillet with rice, soy sauce and sesame seeds; cook and stir 2 minutes or until well blended and heated through. Season with additional salt and pepper; garnish with additional green onion.

Makes 4 servings

MEXICAN CAULIFLOWER AND BEAN SKILLET

- 1 tablespoon olive oil
- 3 cups coarsely chopped cauliflower
- ¾ teaspoon salt
- ½ medium yellow onion, chopped
- 1 green bell pepper, chopped
- 1 clove garlic, minced
- 1 teaspoon chili powder
- ¾ teaspoon ground cumin
- Pinch ground red pepper
- 1 can (about 15 ounces) black beans, rinsed and drained
- 1 cup (4 ounces) shredded Cheddar-Jack cheese
- Salsa and sour cream

1. Heat oil in large nonstick skillet over medium-high heat. Add cauliflower and salt; cook and stir 5 minutes. Add onion, bell pepper, garlic, chili powder, cumin and red pepper; cook and stir 5 minutes or until cauliflower is tender. Stir in beans; cook until beans are heated through. Remove from heat.
2. Sprinkle with cheese; fold in gently and let stand until melted. Serve with salsa and sour cream.

Makes 4 to 6 servings

Serving suggestion: Serve over brown rice or with warm corn tortillas.

MUSHROOM AND CHICKEN SKILLET

- 1 pound boneless skinless chicken breasts, cut into bite-size pieces
- 1 can (about 14 ounces) chicken broth
- ¼ cup water
- 2 cups uncooked instant rice
- ½ teaspoon dried thyme
- 8 ounces mushrooms, thinly sliced
- 1 can (10¾ ounces) cream of celery soup, undiluted
- Chopped fresh parsley (optional)

1. Combine chicken, broth and water in large skillet; bring to a boil over high heat. Stir in rice and thyme; mix well.
2. Sprinkle mushrooms over rice mixture. (Do not stir mushrooms into rice.) Cover skillet; turn off heat and let stand 5 minutes.
3. Stir in soup; cook over low heat 5 minutes or until heated through. Sprinkle with parsley, if desired.

Makes 4 servings

WINTER SQUASH RISOTTO

- **2 tablespoons olive oil**
- **1 small butternut squash or medium delicata squash, peeled and cut into 1-inch pieces (about 2 cups)**
- **1 large shallot or small onion, finely chopped**
- **½ teaspoon salt**
- **½ teaspoon paprika**
- **¼ teaspoon dried thyme**
- **¼ teaspoon black pepper**
- **1 cup uncooked arborio rice**
- **¼ cup dry white wine (optional)**
- **4 to 5 cups hot vegetable broth**
- **½ cup grated Parmesan or Romano cheese**

1. Heat oil in large nonstick skillet over medium heat. Add squash; cook and stir 3 minutes. Add shallot; cook and stir 3 to 4 minutes or until squash is almost tender. Stir in salt, paprika, thyme and pepper. Add rice; stir to coat.
2. Add wine, if desired; cook and stir until wine is absorbed. Add broth, ½ cup at a time, stirring frequently until broth is absorbed before adding next ½ cup. Continue adding broth and stirring until rice is tender and mixture is creamy, about 20 to 25 minutes.
3. Sprinkle with cheese just before serving.

Makes 4 to 6 servings

CANNELLINI CHICKEN SKILLET

- **2 tablespoons olive oil**
- **1 pound boneless skinless chicken breasts, cut into 1-inch pieces**
- **1 can (about 14 ounces) diced tomatoes**
- **1 cup frozen chopped spinach**
- **2 cloves garlic, minced**
- **1 tablespoon chopped fresh rosemary *or* 1 teaspoon dried rosemary**
- **1 teaspoon salt**
- **¼ teaspoon red pepper flakes**
- **1 can (about 15 ounces) cannellini beans, rinsed and drained**
- **1 cup grape tomatoes, cut in half**

1. Heat oil in large skillet over medium-high heat. Add chicken; cook and stir 5 minutes or until lightly browned.
2. Add diced tomatoes, spinach, garlic, rosemary, salt and red pepper flakes; cook over medium heat 10 minutes or until spinach is thawed, stirring frequently.
3. Add beans and grape tomatoes; cook about 3 minutes or until beans are heated through.

Makes 4 servings

CAJUN RICE

- 2 cups uncooked long grain rice
- 4 cups water, divided
- 1¼ teaspoons salt, divided
- 4 green onions, finely chopped, green and white parts separated
- 8 ounces ground beef
- 8 ounces chicken gizzards, minced*
- ½ cup finely chopped green bell pepper
- 1 teaspoon Cajun or Creole seasoning
- ½ teaspoon garlic powder
- ¼ teaspoon celery seed
- ¼ teaspoon ground red pepper
- ¼ teaspoon black pepper

**Or substitute an additional 8 ounces ground beef for the chicken gizzards.*

1. Rinse rice in strainer under cool water; drain. Combine rice, 3¾ cups water and 1 teaspoon salt in medium saucepan; bring to a boil over medium-high heat. Reduce heat to low; cover and cook about 17 minutes or until liquid is absorbed and rice is tender but still firm. Remove from heat; let stand, covered, 5 minutes. Fluff rice with fork; stir in green parts of green onions.

2. Meanwhile, cook beef in large skillet over medium-high heat about 5 minutes or until no longer pink, stirring to break up meat. Remove to plate; drain fat.

3. Add chicken gizzards and bell pepper to skillet; cook 7 minutes or until chicken is cooked through. Add white parts of green onions, Cajun seasoning, garlic powder, celery seed, red pepper, black pepper and remaining ¼ teaspoon salt; cook and stir 2 minutes. Return beef to skillet; mix well.

4. Stir in rice and remaining ¼ cup water; cook over medium-low heat 15 minutes, stirring occasionally.

Makes 8 to 10 servings

Skillet Stir-Fries

BEEF WITH SNOW PEAS AND BABY CORN

- 12 ounces ground beef
- 1 clove garlic, minced
- 1 tablespoon vegetable oil
- 6 ounces snow peas, halved lengthwise
- 1 red bell pepper, cut into thin strips
- 1 can (15 ounces) baby corn, rinsed and drained
- 1 tablespoon soy sauce
- 1 teaspoon dark sesame oil
- Salt and black pepper
- Hot cooked rice

1. Cook beef and garlic in large skillet 6 to 8 minutes over medium-high heat or until browned, stirring to break up meat. Remove to medium bowl. Drain fat.

2. Add vegetable oil to skillet; heat over medium-high heat. Add snow peas and bell pepper; stir-fry 2 to 3 minutes or until vegetables are crisp-tender.

3. Stir in beef mixture, baby corn, soy sauce and sesame oil; cook 2 minutes or until heated through. Season with salt and black pepper. Serve over rice.

Makes 4 servings

MA PO TOFU

- 1 package (14 ounces) firm tofu, drained and pressed*
- 2 tablespoons soy sauce
- 2 teaspoons minced fresh ginger
- 1 cup vegetable broth, divided
- 2 tablespoons black bean sauce
- 1 tablespoon Thai sweet chili sauce
- 1 tablespoon cornstarch
- 2 tablespoons vegetable oil
- 1 green bell pepper, cut into bite-size pieces
- 2 cloves garlic, minced
- 1½ cups broccoli florets
- ¼ cup chopped fresh cilantro (optional)
- Hot cooked rice

**Cut tofu in half horizontally and place it between layers of paper towels. Place weighted cutting board on top; let stand 15 to 30 minutes.*

1. Cut tofu into cubes. Place in shallow dish; sprinkle with soy sauce and ginger.
2. Whisk ¼ cup broth, black bean sauce, chili sauce and cornstarch in small bowl until smooth.
3. Heat oil in large skillet over high heat. Add bell pepper and garlic; stir-fry 2 minutes. Add remaining ¾ cup broth and broccoli; bring to a boil. Reduce heat to medium-low; cover and simmer 3 minutes or until broccoli is crisp-tender.
4. Stir cornstarch mixture; add to skillet. Cook 1 minute or until sauce boils and thickens. Stir in tofu; cook until heated through. Sprinkle with cilantro, if desired. Serve with rice.

Makes 4 servings

MONGOLIAN BEEF

- 1¼ pounds beef flank steak
- ¼ cup cornstarch
- 3 tablespoons vegetable oil, divided
- 3 cloves garlic, minced
- 2 teaspoons grated fresh ginger
- ½ cup water
- ½ cup soy sauce
- ⅓ cup packed dark brown sugar
- Pinch red pepper flakes
- 2 green onions, diagonally sliced into 1-inch pieces
- Hot cooked rice

1. Cut flank steak in half lengthwise, then cut crosswise (against the grain) into ¼-inch slices. Combine beef and cornstarch in medium bowl; toss to coat.
2. Heat 1 tablespoon oil in large skillet over high heat. Add half of beef in single layer (do not crowd); cook 1 to 2 minutes per side or until browned. Remove to clean bowl. Repeat with remaining beef and 1 tablespoon oil.
3. Heat remaining 1 tablespoon oil in skillet over medium heat. Add garlic and ginger; cook and stir 30 seconds. Add water, soy sauce, brown sugar and red pepper flakes; bring to a boil, stirring until well blended. Cook 8 minutes or until sauce is slightly thickened, stirring occasionally.
4. Return beef to skillet; cook 2 to 3 minutes or until sauce thickens and beef is heated through. Stir in green onions. Serve with rice.

Makes 4 servings

PINEAPPLE BASIL CHICKEN

- 1 can (8 ounces) pineapple chunks in unsweetened juice
- 2 teaspoons cornstarch
- 2 tablespoons peanut oil
- 1 pound boneless skinless chicken breasts, cut into ¾-inch pieces
- 2 to 4 serrano peppers, cut into thin strips (optional)
- 2 cloves garlic, minced
- 2 green onions, cut into 1-inch pieces
- ¾ cup roasted unsalted cashew nuts
- ¼ cup chopped fresh basil (do not use dried)
- 1 tablespoon fish sauce
- 1 tablespoon soy sauce
- Hot cooked rice

1. Drain pineapple, reserving juice. Stir reserved juice into cornstarch in small bowl until smooth.
2. Heat large skillet over high heat 1 minute. Add oil; heat 30 seconds. Add chicken, serrano peppers, if desired, and garlic; stir-fry 3 minutes or until chicken is cooked through. Add green onions; stir-fry 1 minute.
3. Stir cornstarch mixture; add to skillet. Cook and stir 1 minute or until sauce thickens. Add pineapple, cashews, basil, fish sauce and soy sauce; cook and stir 1 minute or until heated through. Serve over rice.

Makes 4 servings

TOFU CAULIFLOWER FRIED RICE

- 3 tablespoons soy sauce
- 1 tablespoon plus 1 teaspoon minced fresh ginger, divided
- 2 teaspoons dark sesame oil
- 1 teaspoon packed brown sugar
- 1 teaspoon rice vinegar
- 1 package (14 ounces) firm tofu, drained and cut into 1-inch cubes
- 2 tablespoons vegetable oil, divided
- 1 yellow or sweet onion, chopped
- 1 carrot, chopped
- ½ cup frozen peas
- 2 cloves garlic, minced
- 1 package (12 ounces) frozen cauliflower rice
- 1 green onion, thinly sliced

1. Whisk soy sauce, 1 tablespoon ginger, sesame oil, brown sugar and vinegar in small bowl until blended. Place tofu in quart-size resealable food storage bag. Pour marinade over tofu; seal bag and turn to coat. Refrigerate 3 hours or overnight.
2. Drain tofu, reserving marinade. Heat 1 tablespoon vegetable oil in large skillet over high heat. Add tofu; stir-fry 3 to 5 minutes or until edges are browned. Transfer to medium bowl.
3. Add remaining 1 tablespoon vegetable oil to skillet; heat over high heat. Add yellow onion and carrot; stir-fry 2 minutes or until softened. Add peas, garlic and remaining 1 teaspoon ginger; cook and stir 2 minutes or until peas are hot.
4. Stir in frozen cauliflower rice and ¼ cup reserved marinade; cook 5 minutes or until heated through. Return tofu to skillet; cook until heated through. Sprinkle with green onion.

Makes 4 servings

SWEET AND SPICY PORK AND VEGETABLES

¼ cup water
2 teaspoons cornstarch
4 tablespoons peanut oil, divided
6 whole dried hot red chile peppers
4 cloves garlic, sliced
1 pork tenderloin (about 12 ounces), thinly sliced
1 large carrot, cut into ¼-inch-thick slices
2 ounces fresh oyster, shiitake or button mushrooms,* cut into halves
1 baby eggplant, thinly sliced
5 ounces fresh snow peas, ends trimmed
3 tablespoons packed brown sugar
2 tablespoons fish sauce
1 tablespoon dark sesame oil
Hot cooked rice

**Or substitute ½ ounce dried shiitake mushrooms, soaked according to package directions.*

1. Stir water into cornstarch in small bowl until well blended and smooth.

2. Heat large skillet over high heat 1 minute. Add 2 tablespoons peanut oil; heat 30 seconds. Add chile peppers and garlic; stir-fry 1 minute. Add pork; stir-fry 3 to 4 minutes or until pork is barely pink in center. Remove mixture to medium bowl.

3. Add remaining 2 tablespoons peanut oil to skillet. Add carrot, mushrooms and eggplant; stir-fry 2 minutes. Add snow peas and pork mixture; stir-fry 1 minute.

4. Stir cornstarch mixture; add to skillet. Cook 1 minute or until sauce thickens. Stir in brown sugar, fish sauce and sesame oil; cook and stir until heated through. Serve with rice.

Makes 4 servings

FIVE-SPICE BEEF AND PEPPERS

1 boneless beef top sirloin steak (about 1 pound)
2½ tablespoons cornstarch, divided
2 tablespoons soy sauce
3 tablespoons vegetable oil, divided
4 medium carrots, cut into matchstick-size pieces (about 2 cups)
3 cups hot cooked rice
1 red bell pepper, cut into 1-inch pieces
1 yellow bell pepper, cut into 1-inch pieces
1 cup chopped onion
¼ to ½ teaspoon red pepper flakes
1½ cups beef broth
1½ tablespoons packed dark brown sugar
1 teaspoon Chinese five-spice powder
½ cup honey-roasted peanuts

1. Cut beef in half lengthwise, then cut crosswise into thin strips. Place in shallow dish. Stir 2 tablespoons cornstarch into soy sauce in small bowl until smooth. Pour mixture over beef; toss to coat.

2. Heat 1 tablespoon oil in large skillet over high heat 1 minute. Add carrots; stir-fry 3 to 4 minutes or until edges begin to brown. Combine carrots and rice in medium bowl; mix well. Cover and set aside until ready to serve.

3. Add 1 tablespoon oil, bell peppers, onion and red pepper flakes to skillet; stir-fry over medium-high heat 4 minutes or until onion is translucent. Remove to large bowl.

4. Heat remaining 1 tablespoon oil in skillet. Add half of beef; stir-fry 2 minutes or until beef is barely pink in center. Add to vegetables in large bowl. Repeat with remaining beef.

5. Whisk broth, brown sugar, five-spice powder and remaining ½ tablespoon cornstarch in small bowl until smooth. Combine sauce and beef mixture in skillet; bring to a boil. Reduce heat to medium-low; cook 2 to 3 minutes or until sauce is slightly thickened. Serve over carrots and rice; sprinkle with peanuts.

Makes 4 servings

EASY SEAFOOD STIR-FRY

- 1 package (1 ounce) dried black Chinese mushrooms*
- ½ cup chicken broth
- 2 tablespoons dry sherry
- 1 tablespoon soy sauce
- 1½ tablespoons cornstarch
- 1 tablespoon vegetable oil, divided
- 8 ounces bay scallops or halved sea scallops
- 4 ounces medium raw shrimp, peeled and deveined
- 2 cloves garlic, minced
- 6 ounces (2 cups) fresh snow peas, cut diagonally into halves
- ¼ cup thinly sliced green onions
- Hot cooked rice

**Or substitute 1½ cups sliced fresh mushrooms and omit step 1.*

1. Place mushrooms in medium bowl. Cover with warm water; let stand 20 to 40 minutes or until softened. Drain and squeeze out excess water. Discard stems; cut caps into thin slices.
2. Whisk broth, sherry and soy sauce into cornstarch in small bowl until smooth.
3. Heat ½ tablespoon oil in large nonstick skillet over medium heat. Add scallops, shrimp and garlic; stir-fry 3 minutes or until seafood is opaque. Remove to plate.
4. Add remaining ½ tablespoon oil to skillet; heat over medium-high heat. Add mushrooms and snow peas; stir-fry 3 minutes or until snow peas are crisp-tender. Stir cornstarch mixture; add to skillet. Cook and stir 2 minutes or until sauce boils and thickens.
5. Return seafood to skillet; cook and stir just until heated through. Sprinkle with green onions; serve with rice.

Makes 4 servings

ASPARAGUS CHICKEN

- 1 egg white
- 2 tablespoons cornstarch, divided
- 5 teaspoons soy sauce, divided
- 2 teaspoons dry sherry
- 1 pound chicken tenders, cut in half crosswise
- ½ cup reduced-sodium chicken broth
- 1 teaspoon sesame oil
- 3 tablespoons vegetable oil, divided
- 2 large carrots, julienned
- 1 package (10 ounces) frozen asparagus, partially thawed and cut into 1½ inch pieces
- 1 green onion, cut diagonally into ½-inch slices
- Hot cooked rice

1. Whisk egg white, 1 tablespoon cornstarch, 2 teaspoons soy sauce and sherry in large bowl until smooth. Add chicken; toss to coat.
2. Whisk broth, remaining 1 tablespoon cornstarch, 3 teaspoons soy sauce and sesame oil in small bowl until smooth.
3. Heat 2 tablespoons vegetable oil in large skillet over high heat. Add chicken; stir-fry 4 minutes or until cooked through. Remove to medium bowl.
4. Add remaining 1 tablespoon vegetable oil to skillet; heat over medium-high heat. Add carrots; stir-fry 3 minutes or until crisp-tender. Add asparagus; stir-fry 1 minute.
5. Stir cornstarch mixture; add to skillet. Cook until sauce boils and thickens. Stir in green onion and chicken; cook until heated through. Serve over rice.

Makes 4 servings

THAI VEGGIE CURRY

- **2 tablespoons vegetable oil**
- **1 onion, quartered and thinly sliced**
- **1 tablespoon Thai red curry paste (or to taste)**
- **1 can (about 13 ounces) unsweetened coconut milk**
- **¼ teaspoon salt**
- **2 red or yellow bell peppers, cut into strips**
- **1½ cups cauliflower and/or broccoli florets**
- **1 cup snow peas**
- **1 package (about 14 ounces) tofu, pressed and cubed**
- **¼ cup slivered fresh basil**
- **Hot cooked jasmine rice**

1. Heat oil in large skillet over medium-high heat. Add onion; stir-fry 2 minutes or until softened. Add curry paste; cook and stir to coat onion. Add coconut milk and salt; bring to a boil, stirring to dissolve curry paste.
2. Add bell peppers and cauliflower; cook over medium heat 4 to 5 minutes or until vegetables are crisp-tender. Stir in snow peas; cook 2 minutes. Gently stir in tofu; cook until heated through.
3. Sprinkle with basil; serve with rice.

Makes 4 to 6 servings

SPICY CHINESE PEPPER STEAK

- 1 boneless beef top sirloin steak (about 1 pound) or tenderloin tips, cut into thin strips
- 1 tablespoon cornstarch
- 3 cloves garlic, minced
- ½ teaspoon red pepper flakes
- 2 tablespoons peanut oil, divided
- 1 green bell pepper, cut into thin strips
- 1 red bell pepper, cut into thin strips
- ¼ cup oyster sauce
- 2 tablespoons soy sauce
- 3 tablespoons chopped fresh cilantro or green onions

1. Combine beef, cornstarch, garlic and red pepper flakes in medium bowl; toss to coat.
2. Heat 1 tablespoon oil in large skillet over medium-high heat. Add bell peppers; stir-fry 3 minutes. Remove to medium bowl. Add remaining 1 tablespoon oil and beef mixture to skillet; stir-fry 4 to 5 minutes or until beef is barely pink in center.
3. Add oyster sauce and soy sauce to skillet; cook and stir 1 minute. Return bell peppers to skillet; cook and stir 1 to 2 minutes or until sauce thickens. Sprinkle with cilantro.

Makes 4 servings

SESAME CHICKEN

- 1 pound boneless skinless chicken breasts or thighs, cut into 1-inch pieces
- ⅔ cup teriyaki sauce, divided
- Sweet and Sour Noodles (recipe follows) or hot cooked rice (optional)
- 2 teaspoons cornstarch
- 1 tablespoon peanut or vegetable oil
- 2 cloves garlic, minced
- 2 green onions, cut into ½-inch slices
- 1 tablespoon sesame seeds, toasted*
- 1 teaspoon dark sesame oil

**To toast sesame seeds, cook and stir in small skillet over medium-low heat 3 minutes or until seeds begin to pop and turn golden.*

1. Combine chicken and ⅓ cup teriyaki sauce in medium bowl; toss to coat. Marinate in refrigerator 15 to 20 minutes. Meanwhile, prepare Sweet and Sour Noodles, if desired.

2. Drain chicken; discard marinade. Stir remaining ⅓ cup teriyaki sauce into cornstarch in small bowl until smooth.

3. Heat peanut oil in large skillet over medium-high heat. Add chicken and garlic; stir-fry 3 minutes or until chicken is cooked through. Stir cornstarch mixture; add to skillet. Cook and stir 1 minute or until sauce boils and thickens. Stir in green onions, sesame seeds and sesame oil. Serve with noodles.

Makes 4 servings

Sweet and Sour Noodles: Whisk ¼ cup teriyaki sauce, 3 tablespoons rice vinegar, 3 cloves minced garlic, 1 tablespoon dark sesame oil and ¼ teaspoon chili oil, if desired, in large bowl. Cook 1 package (10 ounces) dried lo mein noodles according to package directions. Drain and add to bowl with sauce; stir to coat. Stir in 1 cup thinly sliced red bell pepper and 3 sliced green onions.

Super Skillet Suppers

BRATWURST SKILLET

- 1 pound bratwurst links, cut into ½-inch slices
- 1½ cups sliced onions
- 1½ cups green bell pepper strips
- 1½ cups red bell pepper strips
- 1 teaspoon paprika
- 1 teaspoon caraway seeds
- ¼ teaspoon salt

1. Heat large skillet over medium heat. Add bratwurst; cover and cook about 5 minutes or until browned and no longer pink in center. Remove to plate; cover to keep warm.
2. Drain off all but 1 tablespoon drippings. Add onions, bell peppers, paprika, caraway seeds and salt to skillet; cook about 5 minutes or until vegetables are tender, stirring occasionally.
3. Return bratwurst to skillet; mix well. Serve immediately.

Makes 4 servings

QUICK CHICKEN AND ZUCCHINI PARM

- **4 boneless skinless chicken breasts (4 to 6 ounces each)**
- **½ teaspoon salt, divided**
- **2 tablespoons olive oil, divided**
- **1 medium onion, chopped**
- **1 small zucchini, sliced**
- **1 jar (26 ounces) pasta sauce**
- **½ teaspoon dried basil**
- **½ teaspoon dried oregano**
- **¼ cup grated Parmesan cheese**
- **8 ounces fresh mozzarella cheese, cut into thin slices**
- **Hot cooked pasta (optional)**

1. Preheat broiler. Sprinkle chicken with ¼ teaspoon salt.
2. Heat 1 tablespoon oil in large broilerproof skillet over medium-high heat. Add chicken; cook 5 to 7 minutes or until browned on both sides. Remove to plate; tent with foil to keep warm.
3. Add remaining 1 tablespoon oil, onion, zucchini and remaining ¼ teaspoon salt to skillet; cook 5 minutes or until vegetables are softened, stirring occasionally. Stir in pasta sauce, basil and oregano. Return chicken to skillet; turn to coat with sauce. Sprinkle chicken with Parmesan; top with mozzarella.
4. Broil 6 inches from heat 5 to 7 minutes or until chicken is no longer pink in center and cheese is beginning to brown. Serve with pasta, if desired.

Makes 4 servings

STEAK FAJITAS

- ¼ cup lime juice
- ¼ cup soy sauce
- 4 tablespoons vegetable oil, divided
- 2 tablespoons honey
- 2 tablespoons Worcestershire sauce
- 2 cloves garlic, minced
- ½ teaspoon ground red pepper
- 1 pound flank steak, skirt steak or top sirloin
- 1 medium yellow onion, halved and cut into ¼-inch slices
- 1 green bell pepper, cut into ¼-inch strips
- 1 red bell pepper, cut into ¼-inch strips
- Flour tortillas, warmed
- Lime wedges (optional)
- Optional toppings: pico de gallo, guacamole, sour cream, shredded lettuce and shredded Cheddar-Jack cheese

1. Whisk lime juice, soy sauce, 2 tablespoons oil, honey, Worcestershire sauce, garlic and ground red pepper in medium bowl until well blended. Remove ¼ cup marinade to large bowl.
2. Place steak in large resealable food storage bag. Pour remaining marinade over steak; seal bag and turn to coat. Marinate in refrigerator at least 2 hours or overnight. Add onion and bell peppers to bowl with ¼ cup marinade; toss to coat. Cover and refrigerate until ready to cook.
3. Remove steak from marinade; discard marinade and pat steak dry with paper towels. Heat 1 tablespoon oil in large skillet (preferably cast iron) over medium-high heat. Cook steak 4 minutes per side for medium rare or until desired doneness. Remove to cutting board; tent with foil and let stand 10 minutes.
4. Meanwhile, heat remaining 1 tablespoon oil in same skillet over medium-high heat. Add vegetable mixture; cook 8 minutes or until vegetables are crisp-tender and beginning to brown in spots, stirring occasionally. (Cook in two batches if necessary; do not crowd skillet.)
5. Cut steak into thin slices across the grain. Serve with vegetables, tortillas, lime wedges and desired toppings.

Makes 2 servings

PORK AND SWEET POTATO SKILLET

- 2 tablespoons butter, divided
- 12 ounces pork tenderloin, cut into 1-inch pieces
- ½ teaspoon salt, divided
- ¼ teaspoon black pepper, divided
- 2 medium sweet potatoes, peeled and cut into ½-inch pieces (about 2 cups)
- 1 small onion, sliced
- 4 ounces smoked turkey sausage, halved lengthwise and cut into ½-inch pieces
- 1 small green or red apple, cut into ½-inch slices
- ½ cup sweet and sour sauce
- 2 tablespoons chopped fresh parsley (optional)

1. Heat 1 tablespoon butter in large skillet over medium-high heat. Add pork; cook and stir 2 to 3 minutes or until no longer pink. Season with ¼ teaspoon salt and ⅛ teaspoon pepper. Remove to plate; tent with foil to keep warm.
2. Add remaining 1 tablespoon butter, sweet potatoes, onion, remaining ¼ teaspoon salt and ⅛ teaspoon pepper to skillet; cover and cook over medium-low heat 8 to 10 minutes or until vegetables are tender.
3. Add pork, sausage, apple and sweet and sour sauce to skillet; cook 5 minutes or until heated through, stirring occasionally. Garnish with parsley.

Makes 4 servings

SHAKSHUKA

- ¼ cup olive oil
- 1 medium onion, chopped
- 1 large red bell pepper, chopped
- 3 cloves garlic, sliced
- 1 can (28 ounces) crushed tomatoes with basil, garlic and oregano
- 2 teaspoons sugar
- 2 teaspoons ground cumin
- 2 teaspoons paprika
- ½ teaspoon salt
- ¼ teaspoon red pepper flakes
- ¾ cup (3 ounces) crumbled feta cheese
- 6 eggs
- Chopped fresh cilantro or parsley (optional)
- Toasted baguette slices or pita bread wedges (optional)

1. Heat oil in large skillet over medium-high heat. Add onion and bell pepper; cook and stir 5 minutes or until vegetables are softened. Add garlic; cook and stir 1 minute. Stir in tomatoes, sugar, cumin, paprika, salt and red pepper flakes; mix well. Reduce heat to medium-low; simmer 25 minutes, stirring frequently. Stir in cheese.
2. Make six divots in tomato sauce; crack one egg into each divot. Cover and cook 15 to 18 minutes or until egg whites are set but yolks are still creamy.
3. Scoop eggs and sauce into serving dishes. Sprinkle with cilantro and serve with bread, if desired.

Makes 6 servings

CHICKEN MARSALA

- **4 boneless skinless chicken breasts (6 to 8 ounces each)**
- **½ cup all-purpose flour**
- **1 teaspoon coarse salt**
- **¼ teaspoon black pepper**
- **2 tablespoons olive oil**
- **3 tablespoons butter, divided**
- **2 cups sliced mushrooms**
- **1 shallot, minced (about 2 tablespoons)**
- **1 clove garlic, minced**
- **1 cup dry Marsala wine**
- **½ cup chicken broth**
- **Finely chopped fresh parsley**

1. Cut chicken breasts in half crosswise. Pound each piece to ¼-inch thickness between two sheets of plastic wrap with meat mallet or rolling pin.
2. Combine flour, salt and pepper in shallow dish. Coat both sides of chicken with flour mixture, shaking off excess.
3. Heat oil and 1 tablespoon butter in large skillet over medium-high heat. Add chicken in single layer; cook about 4 minutes per side or until golden brown. Remove to plate; tent with foil to keep warm.
4. Add 1 tablespoon butter, mushrooms and shallot to skillet; cook 10 minutes or until mushrooms are deep golden brown, stirring occasionally. Add garlic; cook and stir 1 minute. Stir in wine and broth; cook 2 minutes, scraping up browned bits from bottom of skillet. Stir in remaining 1 tablespoon butter until melted.
5. Return chicken to skillet; turn to coat with sauce. Cook 2 minutes or until heated through. Sprinkle with parsley.

Makes 4 servings

STOVETOP SHEPHERD'S PIE

- 1 tablespoon olive oil
- 8 ounces ground turkey
- 1 cup chopped onion
- 1 cup chopped green bell pepper
- 1⅔ cups water, divided
- 3 tablespoons ketchup
- 1 tablespoon Worcestershire sauce
- ¼ teaspoon ground cumin
- ⅛ teaspoon ground red pepper
- ¼ teaspoon salt
- 1¼ cups milk
- 1⅓ cups instant mashed potatoes
- ½ cup (2 ounces) shredded sharp Cheddar cheese

1. Heat oil in medium skillet over medium-high heat. Add turkey; cook 6 to 8 minutes or until browned, stirring to break up meat. Remove to small bowl; drain off any excess liquid, if necessary.

2. Add onion and bell pepper to skillet; cook and stir over medium-high heat 5 minutes or until onion is softened. Add turkey, ⅓ cup water, ketchup, Worcestershire sauce, cumin and red pepper; cook and stir 2 minutes or until slightly thickened. Remove from heat.

3. Meanwhile, bring remaining 1⅓ cups water and salt to a boil in medium saucepan. Remove from heat; stir in milk and potatoes. Spread mashed potatoes evenly over turkey mixture; sprinkle with cheese.

4. Return skillet to medium-low heat; cover and cook 6 to 8 minutes or until cheese is melted.

Makes 6 servings

PORK SCHNITZEL WITH MUSHROOM GRAVY

- **6 thin-cut boneless pork sirloin chops or boneless pork loin chops (about 1½ pounds)***
- **Salt and black pepper**
- **½ cup plus 1 tablespoon all-purpose flour, divided**
- **2 eggs**
- **1 cup plain dry bread crumbs**
- **2 tablespoons chopped fresh parsley *or* 1 tablespoon dried parsley flakes**
- **2 tablespoons vegetable oil**
- **4 tablespoons (½ stick) butter, divided**
- **¼ cup finely chopped onion**
- **1 package (8 ounces) sliced mushrooms**
- **1 cup chicken broth**
- **2 to 3 tablespoons half-and-half**

****Or substitute pork cutlets for the boneless pork chops.***

1. Pound pork chops to ⅛-inch thickness with meat mallet or rolling pin. Season with salt and pepper. Place ½ cup flour in shallow dish. Beat eggs in separate shallow dish. Combine bread crumbs and parsley in third shallow dish.
2. Coat pork chops with flour, shaking off excess. Dip in eggs, then in bread crumb mixture, turning to coat.
3. Heat oil and 2 tablespoons butter in large skillet over medium heat. Cook pork chops in two batches about 3 minutes per side or until browned. *Do not overcook.* Remove to plate; tent with foil to keep warm.
4. Melt remaining 2 tablespoons butter in same skillet over medium heat. Add onion; cook and stir 1 minute. Add mushrooms; cook and stir 6 to 7 minutes or until mushrooms are lightly browned and most of liquid has evaporated. Add remaining 1 tablespoon flour; cook and stir 1 minute. Add broth; bring to a boil, stirring constantly. Boil 1 minute. Remove from heat; stir in half-and-half.
5. Spoon gravy over pork. Serve immediately.

Makes 6 servings

TOFU IN PURGATORY

- 2 tablespoons olive oil
- 1 large onion, chopped
- 2 cloves garlic, minced
- 2 tablespoons tomato paste
- 1 teaspoon salt
- 1 teaspoon ground cumin
- 1 teaspoon ground coriander
- ½ teaspoon smoked paprika
- 1 can (28 ounces) diced tomatoes
- Crispy Toast (optional, recipe follows)
- 1 package (about 12 ounces) firm silken tofu, cut into 8 cubes
- Shredded fresh basil (optional)

1. Heat oil in large skillet over medium-high heat. Add onion; cook and stir 5 minutes or until softened. Add garlic, tomato paste, salt, cumin, coriander and paprika; cook and stir 1 minute.
2. Stir in tomatoes; bring to a simmer. Reduce heat to medium-low; cook 20 minutes, stirring occasionally. Meanwhile, prepare Crispy Toast, if desired.
3. Make eight divots in sauce. Add tofu cubes; cover and cook 10 minutes to heat tofu. Scoop into bowls; garnish with basil and serve with toast.

Makes 4 servings

Crispy Toast: Preheat oven to 400°F. Place 4 to 8 slices of French, Italian or sourdough bread on baking sheet; brush both sides of bread with olive oil. Bake 8 to 10 minutes or until golden brown and crisp, turning once. Cut 2 garlic cloves in half; rub cut sides over one side of each toast slice.

CHICKEN PICADILLO

- 1 tablespoon olive oil
- 1 medium onion, chopped
- 1 green bell pepper, chopped
- 1 small hot chile pepper, seeded and chopped
- 1 pound ground chicken
- 2 cloves garlic, minced
- 1 can (14 ounces) diced tomatoes
- ¼ cup raisins
- ¼ cup sliced pimiento-stuffed green olives
- 1 tablespoon capers (optional)
- ½ teaspoon salt
- ¼ teaspoon ground cumin
- ¼ teaspoon black pepper
- Hot cooked rice

1. Heat oil in large skillet over medium heat. Add onion, bell pepper and chile pepper; cook and stir 3 minutes or until onion is crisp-tender. Add chicken and garlic; cook 5 minutes, stirring to break up chicken.

2. Stir in tomatoes, raisins, olives, capers, if desired, salt, cumin and pepper; simmer 20 minutes, stirring occasionally. Serve over rice.

Makes 4 servings

BALSAMIC-GLAZED SIRLOIN AND SPINACH

- **5 tablespoons olive oil, divided**
- **2 Vidalia or other sweet onions, thinly sliced**
- **3 tablespoons balsamic vinegar, divided**
- **1¼ teaspoons salt, divided**
- **1 teaspoon black pepper**
- **1 pound top sirloin steak (1 inch thick)**
- **1 package (8 to 10 ounces) fresh spinach, coarsely chopped**

1. Heat 2 tablespoons oil in large skillet over medium-high heat. Add onions; cook 10 minutes or until softened, stirring occasionally. Sprinkle with 1 tablespoon vinegar and ½ teaspoon salt; cook 10 minutes or until beginning to brown. Remove to medium bowl; cover to keep warm.
2. Meanwhile, press pepper into both sides of steak. Sprinkle with ½ teaspoon vinegar and ½ teaspoon salt.
3. Heat 1 tablespoon oil in same skillet over medium-high heat. Add steak; cook 5 minutes. Turn and cook 3 to 5 minutes for medium rare (135°F) or until desired doneness. Remove to cutting board; tent with foil and let stand 5 minutes before slicing.
4. Add remaining 2 tablespoons oil to skillet. Add spinach; cover and cook 2 minutes. Stir spinach; cook 1 minute if necessary to wilt all of spinach. Add remaining vinegar and ¼ teaspoon salt; cook and stir 1 minute.
5. Cut steak into thin slices; serve over spinach and onions.

Makes 4 servings

PORK CHOPS WITH VINEGAR PEPPERS

- **4 pork rib chops (about 1 inch thick)**
- **½ teaspoon salt**
- **¼ teaspoon black pepper**
- **2 tablespoons olive oil**
- **1½ cups seeded hot cherry peppers, cut into ½-inch slices***
- **2 cloves garlic, minced**
- **¼ cup liquid from cherry pepper jar**
- **¼ cup water**
- **1 sprig fresh rosemary**

****Hot cherry peppers are also available presliced in rings.***

1. Pat pork chops dry with paper towels. Season both sides of pork chops with salt and black pepper.
2. Heat oil in large skillet over medium-high heat. Add pork chops; cook about 5 minutes per side or until browned. Remove to plate.
3. Add cherry peppers and garlic to skillet; cook and stir 2 minutes over medium heat, scraping up browned bits from bottom of skillet. Stir in cherry pepper liquid, water and rosemary.
4. Return pork chops to skillet; cover and cook about 6 minutes or until pork is barely pink in center.

Makes 4 servings

PUMPKIN CURRY

- 1 tablespoon vegetable oil
- 1 package (14 ounces) firm tofu, drained, patted dry and cut into 1-inch cubes
- ¼ cup Thai red curry paste
- 2 cloves garlic, minced
- 1 can (15 ounces) pure pumpkin
- 1 can (about 13 ounces) coconut milk
- 1 cup vegetable broth or water
- 1½ teaspoons salt
- 1 teaspoon sriracha sauce
- 4 cups cut-up fresh vegetables (broccoli, cauliflower, red bell pepper and/or sweet potato)
- ½ cup peas
- Hot cooked rice
- ¼ cup shredded fresh basil (optional)

1. Heat oil in large skillet over high heat. Add tofu; cook and stir 5 minutes or until lightly browned. Add curry paste and garlic; cook and stir 1 minute or until tofu is coated.

2. Stir in pumpkin, coconut milk, broth, salt and sriracha; bring to a boil. Stir in vegetables. Reduce heat to medium; cover and simmer 20 minutes or until vegetables are tender.

3. Stir in peas; cook 1 minute or until heated through. Serve with rice; sprinkle with basil, if desired.

Makes 4 servings

SHERRIED BEEF STEW

- 1 tablespoon butter
- 1½ pounds boneless chuck roast, cut into 1-inch pieces
- 2 cups beef broth
- 1 medium onion, cut into 8 wedges
- 4 ounces medium mushrooms, quartered
- 4 cloves garlic, minced
- 1 teaspoon salt, divided
- 12 ounces baking potatoes, cut into 1-inch pieces
- ½ cup whipping cream
- 1½ tablespoons cornstarch
- ¼ cup sherry
- 2 tablespoons chopped fresh oregano
- ¼ teaspoon black pepper
- 2 tablespoons chopped fresh parsley

1. Melt butter in large skillet over medium-high heat. Add half of beef; cook and stir 3 to 4 minutes or until beef begins to brown. Remove to plate. Repeat with remaining beef.
2. Stir in broth, scraping up browned bits from bottom of skillet. Return beef to skillet with onion, mushrooms, garlic and ¾ teaspoon salt; bring to a boil over high heat. Reduce heat to low, cover and simmer 1 hour or until beef is tender. Add potatoes; cover and cook 15 to 20 minutes or until potatoes are tender.
3. Whisk cream into cornstarch in small bowl until smooth.
4. Add cornstarch mixture, sherry, oregano, remaining ¼ teaspoon salt and pepper to skillet; bring to a boil over high heat. Boil 1 minute or until stew is thickened, stirring constantly. Sprinkle with parsley.

Makes 4 servings

BBQ CHICKEN SKILLET PIZZA

- 1 loaf (16 ounces) frozen bread dough, thawed according to package directions
- 1 tablespoon olive oil
- 2 cups shredded cooked chicken*
- ¾ cup barbecue sauce, divided
- ¼ cup (1 ounce) shredded mozzarella cheese
- ¼ cup thinly sliced red onion
- ½ cup (2 ounces) shredded smoked Gouda cheese
- Chopped fresh cilantro (optional)

**Use a rotisserie chicken for best flavor and convenience.*

1. Preheat oven to 425°F. Roll out dough into 15-inch circle on lightly floured surface. Brush oil over bottom and side of large (12-inch) ovenproof skillet; place in oven 5 minutes to preheat.
2. Combine chicken and ½ cup barbecue sauce in medium bowl; toss to coat. Remove hot skillet from oven; press dough into bottom and about 1 inch up side of skillet.
3. Spread remaining ¼ cup barbecue sauce over dough. Sprinkle with mozzarella; top with chicken mixture. Sprinkle with half of onion and Gouda; top with remaining onion.
4. Bake 25 minutes or until crust is golden brown. Garnish with cilantro.

Makes 4 to 6 servings

Simple Skillet Sides

BRUSSELS SPROUTS WITH BACON, THYME AND RAISINS

- **1 pound Brussels sprouts**
- **½ cup chicken broth**
- **¼ teaspoon salt**
- **⅓ cup golden raisins**
- **1 thick slice applewood smoked bacon, chopped**
- **1 tablespoon chopped fresh thyme**

1. Trim ends from Brussels sprouts; cut in half lengthwise (or in quarters if large).
2. Combine Brussels sprouts, broth and salt in large skillet; bring to a boil over high heat. Reduce heat to low; cover and simmer 5 minutes.
3. Add raisins; cook, uncovered, 4 to 5 minutes or until broth is absorbed. Add bacon; cook and stir 3 to 4 minutes or until Brussels sprouts are tender. Stir in thyme.

Makes 4 servings

BUTTERNUT SQUASH IN COCONUT MILK

- ⅓ cup flaked coconut
- 2 teaspoons vegetable oil
- ½ small onion, finely chopped
- 2 cloves garlic, minced
- 1 cup unsweetened coconut milk
- ¼ cup packed brown sugar
- 1 tablespoon fish sauce or soy sauce
- ¼ teaspoon salt
- ⅛ to ¼ teaspoon red pepper flakes
- 1 butternut squash (2 to 2½ pounds), peeled and cut into large cubes
- 1 tablespoon chopped fresh cilantro

1. Cook coconut in large skillet over medium-low heat 5 to 7 minutes or until lightly browned, stirring frequently. Remove to plate to cool completely.
2. Add oil to skillet; heat over medium-high heat. Add onion and garlic; cook and stir 3 minutes or until tender. Add coconut milk, brown sugar, fish sauce, salt and red pepper flakes; stir until brown sugar is dissolved. Bring to a boil; stir in squash.
3. Reduce heat to medium; cover and simmer 30 minutes or until squash is tender. Transfer squash to serving bowl with slotted spoon.
4. Increase heat to high; boil liquid remaining in skillet until thick, stirring constantly. Pour liquid over squash in bowl; stir gently to blend. Sprinkle with toasted coconut and cilantro.

Makes 4 to 6 servings

CREAMY PARMESAN SPINACH

- **2 tablespoons butter, divided**
- **1 cup finely chopped yellow onion**
- **2 packages (8 to 10 ounces each) fresh spinach, divided**
- **3 ounces cream cheese, cut into pieces**
- **½ teaspoon salt**
- **½ teaspoon garlic powder**
- **¼ teaspoon ground nutmeg**
- **¼ teaspoon black pepper**
- **2 tablespoons grated Parmesan, pecorino or Monterey Jack cheese**

1. Melt 1 tablespoon butter in large skillet over medium-high heat. Add onion; cook and stir 4 minutes or until translucent.
2. Add 1 package spinach; cook and stir 2 minutes or just until wilted. Remove to medium bowl; repeat with remaining 1 tablespoon butter and spinach.
3. Return reserved spinach to skillet. Add cream cheese, salt, garlic powder, nutmeg and pepper; cook and stir until cream cheese has completely melted.
4. Sprinkle with Parmesan just before serving.

Makes 4 to 6 servings

Tip: For a thinner consistency, add 2 to 3 tablespoons milk before adding the Parmesan cheese.

SKILLET ROASTED ROOT VEGETABLES

- **1 sweet potato, peeled, cut in half lengthwise and cut crosswise into ½-inch slices**
- **1 large red onion, cut into 1-inch wedges**
- **2 parsnips, cut diagonally into 1-inch slices**
- **2 carrots, cut diagonally into 1-inch slices**
- **1 turnip, peeled, cut in half and cut into ½-inch slices**
- **2½ tablespoons olive oil**
- **1½ tablespoons honey**
- **1½ tablespoons balsamic vinegar**
- **1 teaspoon coarse salt**
- **1 teaspoon dried thyme**
- **¼ teaspoon ground red pepper**
- **¼ teaspoon black pepper**

1. Preheat oven to 400°F.
2. Combine all ingredients in large bowl; toss to coat. Spread vegetables evenly in large ovenproof skillet.
3. Roast 1 hour or until vegetables are tender, stirring halfway through cooking.

Makes 4 servings

BUCKWHEAT WITH ZUCCHINI AND MUSHROOMS

- 2 tablespoons olive oil
- 1 cup sliced mushrooms
- 1 medium zucchini, cut into ½-inch pieces
- 1 medium onion, chopped
- 1 clove garlic, minced
- ¾ cup buckwheat
- ¾ teaspoon salt
- ¼ teaspoon dried thyme
- ⅛ teaspoon black pepper
- 1¼ cups vegetable broth
- Lemon wedges (optional)

1. Heat oil in large skillet over medium heat. Add mushrooms, zucchini, onion and garlic; cook and stir 7 to 10 minutes or until vegetables are tender. Add buckwheat, salt, thyme and pepper; cook and stir 2 minutes.

2. Stir in broth; bring to a boil. Reduce heat to low; cover and simmer 10 to 13 minutes or until liquid is absorbed and buckwheat is tender. Remove from heat; let stand, covered, 5 minutes. Serve with lemon wedges, if desired.

Makes 6 servings

Variation: For a different flavor, add pancetta to this dish. Coarsely chop 4 slices pancetta and cook in large skillet over medium heat about 5 minutes to render fat. Add 1 tablespoon olive oil, mushrooms, zucchini, onion and garlic. Proceed as directed above.

CRISPY SKILLET POTATOES

- 2 tablespoons olive oil
- 4 unpeeled red potatoes, cut into thin wedges
- ½ cup chopped onion
- 2 tablespoons lemon pepper seasoning
- ½ teaspoon coarse salt
- Chopped fresh parsley (optional)

1. Heat oil in large skillet over medium heat. Stir in potatoes, onion, lemon pepper seasoning and salt; cover and cook 25 to 30 minutes or until potatoes are tender and browned, turning occasionally.
2. Sprinkle with parsley, if desired, just before serving.

Makes 4 servings

COUNTRY-STYLE CORN

- 4 slices bacon
- 1 tablespoon all-purpose flour
- 1 can (about 15 ounces) corn, drained
- 1 can (about 15 ounces) cream-style corn
- 1 red bell pepper, diced
- ½ cup sliced green onions
- Salt and black pepper

1. Cook bacon in large skillet over medium heat until crisp. Remove to paper towel-lined plate. Crumble bacon; set aside.
2. Whisk flour into drippings in skillet. Add corn, cream-style corn and bell pepper; bring to a boil. Reduce heat to low; cook 10 minutes or until thickened, stirring occasionally.
3. Stir in green onions and bacon. Season with salt and black pepper.

Makes 6 to 8 servings

RED CABBAGE WITH BACON AND MUSHROOMS

- 5 slices thick-cut bacon, chopped (about 8 ounces)
- 1 onion, chopped
- 1 package (8 ounces) cremini mushrooms, chopped (½-inch pieces)
- ¾ teaspoon dried thyme
- ½ medium red cabbage, cut into wedges, cored and cut crosswise into ¼-inch slices (about 7 cups)
- ¼ teaspoon salt
- ¼ teaspoon black pepper
- ⅔ cup chicken broth
- 3 tablespoons cider vinegar
- ¼ cup chopped walnuts, toasted*
- 3 tablespoons chopped fresh parsley

**To toast walnuts, cook in small skillet over medium heat 4 to 5 minutes or until lightly browned, stirring frequently.*

1. Cook bacon in large skillet over medium-high heat until crisp. Remove to paper towel-lined plate. Drain all but 1 tablespoon drippings from skillet.
2. Add onion to skillet; cook and stir 5 minutes or until softened. Add mushrooms and thyme; cook 6 minutes or until mushrooms begin to brown, stirring occasionally. Add cabbage, salt and pepper; cook 7 minutes or until cabbage is wilted.
3. Stir in broth, vinegar and half of bacon; bring to a boil. Reduce heat to low; cook 15 to 20 minutes or until cabbage is tender, stirring occasionally.
4. Stir in walnuts and parsley; season with additional salt and pepper, if desired. Sprinkle with remaining bacon.

Makes 6 servings

MEXICAN RICE

- 1¾ cups vegetable broth or water, divided
- 1 can (8 ounces) tomato sauce
- ½ medium onion, chopped
- 2 teaspoons salt
- 1 clove garlic
- ¾ teaspoon ground cumin
- 2 tablespoons vegetable oil
- 1 cup long grain rice, rinsed well in fine-mesh strainer
- ½ cup frozen peas
- 1 carrot, diced

1. Combine ¼ cup broth, tomato sauce, onion, salt, garlic and cumin in blender; blend until smooth.
2. Heat oil in medium skillet over medium-high heat. Add rice; cook about 6 minutes or until lightly browned, stirring frequently. Add tomato mixture; cook and stir 5 minutes.
3. Stir in remaining 1½ cups broth, peas and carrot; bring to a boil. Reduce heat to low; cover and cook 15 minutes or until rice and carrot are tender.

Makes 4 to 6 servings

CINNAMON APPLES

- ¼ cup (½ stick) butter
- 3 tart red apples such as Gala, Fuji or Honeycrisp (about 1½ pounds total), peeled and cut into ½-inch wedges
- ¼ cup packed brown sugar
- 1 teaspoon ground cinnamon
- ⅛ teaspoon ground nutmeg
- ⅛ teaspoon salt
- 1 tablespoon cornstarch

1. Melt butter in large skillet over medium-high heat. Add apples; cook 8 minutes or until tender, stirring occasionally.
2. Add brown sugar, cinnamon, nutmeg and salt; cook and stir 1 minute or until apples are glazed. Reduce heat to medium-low; stir in cornstarch until well blended.
3. Remove from heat; let stand 5 minutes for glaze to thicken. Stir again; serve immediately.

Makes 4 servings

GREEN BEANS AND MUSHROOMS

- **1½ tablespoons olive oil, divided**
- **1 small onion, thinly sliced**
- **8 ounces sliced mushrooms**
- **¾ teaspoon salt, divided**
- **1 pound fresh green beans, trimmed**
- **1 teaspoon minced garlic**
- **¼ teaspoon black pepper**

1. Heat 1 tablespoon oil in large skillet over medium-high heat. Add onion; cook and stir 2 minutes or until beginning to soften. Add mushrooms; cook about 5 minutes or until mushrooms release their liquid and begin to brown, stirring occasionally.
2. Add beans, remaining ½ tablespoon oil and ½ teaspoon salt to skillet; cook and stir 3 minutes. Reduce heat to medium-low; cover and cook 10 to 12 minutes or until beans are crisp-tender.
3. Stir in garlic, remaining ¼ teaspoon salt and pepper; cook and stir 2 minutes.

Makes 4 to 6 servings

SKILLET SUCCOTASH

- 1 tablespoon vegetable oil
- ½ cup diced onion
- ½ cup diced green bell pepper
- ½ cup diced celery
- ½ teaspoon paprika
- ¾ cup frozen yellow or white corn
- ¾ cup frozen lima beans
- ½ cup canned diced tomatoes
- 1 teaspoon dried parsley flakes *or* 1 tablespoon minced fresh parsley
- ¾ teaspoon salt
- ¼ teaspoon black pepper

1. Heat oil in large skillet over medium heat. Add onion, bell pepper and celery; cook and stir 5 minutes or until onion is translucent and bell pepper and celery are crisp-tender. Add paprika; cook and stir 1 minute.
2. Stir in corn, lima beans and tomatoes, parsley flakes, salt and black pepper; cover and simmer over low heat 20 minutes or until beans are tender.

Makes 4 servings

Tip: For additional flavor, add 1 clove minced garlic and 1 bay leaf in step 2. Remove and discard bay leaf before serving.

JALAPEÑO BLACK BEAN SKILLET

- ¾ cup instant white rice
- 1 can (about 15 ounces) black beans, rinsed and drained
- 1 ounce pickled jalapeño peppers, chopped
- ¼ teaspoon salt
- ½ cup (2 ounces) shredded Mexican blend cheese
- ¼ cup chopped fresh cilantro
- ½ cup sour cream

1. Cook rice in large skillet according to package directions.
2. Stir in beans, pickled jalapeños and salt; mix well. Sprinkle with cheese; cover and cook over medium-low heat 5 minutes or until cheese is melted. Sprinkle with cilantro; serve with sour cream.

Makes 4 servings

SAUTÉED KALE WITH MUSHROOMS AND BACON

- 1 slice bacon, chopped
- ½ cup sliced shallots
- 1 package (8 ounces) sliced mixed fresh mushrooms *or* 8 ounces cremini mushrooms, sliced
- 10 cups loosely packed torn stemmed kale (about 8 ounces)
- 2 tablespoons water
- ¼ teaspoon salt
- ½ teaspoon black pepper

1. Cook bacon in large skillet over medium heat 5 minutes. Add shallots; cook and stir 3 minutes. Add mushrooms; cook and stir 8 minutes.
2. Add kale, water and salt; cover and cook 5 minutes. Uncover; cook 5 minutes or until kale is crisp-tender, stirring frequently. Season with pepper.

Makes 4 servings

Sweet & Savory Skillet Bakes

AUSTRALIAN DAMPER BREAD

- 3 cups self-rising flour
- 1 teaspoon salt
- 6 tablespoons (¾ stick) cold butter, cut into pieces
- 1½ cups milk

1. Preheat oven to 375°F. Line 9-inch cast iron skillet with parchment paper.
2. Combine flour and salt in medium bowl. Add butter; mix with fingers, squeezing butter into flour until coarse crumbs form. Stir in milk until dough forms.
3. Turn out dough onto floured surface; pat into 9-inch circle with floured or dampened hands. Place dough in prepared skillet; score deep X shape into top of dough with sharp knife.
4. Bake about 25 minutes or until top is lightly browned and toothpick inserted into center comes out clean.

Makes 6 to 8 servings

SPANIKOPITA PULL-APARTS

- **4 tablespoons (½ stick) butter, melted, divided**
- **12 frozen white dinner rolls (⅓ of 3-pound package),* thawed according to package directions**
- **1 package (10 ounces) frozen chopped spinach, thawed and squeezed dry**
- **4 green onions, finely chopped (about ¼ cup packed)**
- **1 clove garlic, minced**
- **1 teaspoon dried dill weed**
- **½ teaspoon salt**
- **⅛ teaspoon black pepper**
- **1 cup (4 ounces) crumbled feta cheese**
- **¾ cup (3 ounces) grated Monterey Jack cheese, divided**

If frozen dinner rolls are not available, substitute one 16-ounce loaf of frozen bread dough or pizza dough. Thaw according to package directions and divide into 12 pieces.

1. Brush large (10-inch) ovenproof skillet with ½ tablespoon butter. Cut rolls in half to make 24 balls of dough.
2. Combine spinach, green onions, garlic, dill weed, salt and pepper in medium bowl; mix well to break apart spinach. Add feta, ½ cup Monterey Jack and remaining 3½ tablespoons butter; mix well.
3. Coat each ball of dough with spinach mixture; arrange in single layer in prepared skillet. Sprinkle any remaining spinach mixture between and over balls of dough. Cover and let rise in warm place about 40 minutes or until almost doubled in size. Preheat oven to 350°F. Sprinkle remaining ¼ cup Monterey Jack over dough.
4. Bake 35 to 40 minutes or until golden brown. Serve warm.

Makes 24 rolls

SAUSAGE AND CHEDDAR CORN BREAD

- 1 tablespoon vegetable oil
- 8 ounces bulk pork sausage
- 1 medium onion, diced
- 1 jalapeño pepper, diced
- 1 package (about 8 ounces) corn muffin mix
- 1 cup (4 ounces) shredded Cheddar cheese, divided
- ⅓ cup milk
- 1 egg

1. Heat oil in large ovenproof skillet over medium heat. Add sausage; cook 6 to 8 minutes or until browned, stirring to break up meat. Add onion and jalapeño; cook and stir 5 minutes or until vegetables are softened. Remove sausage mixture to medium bowl.

2. Preheat oven to 350°F. Combine corn muffin mix, ½ cup cheese, milk and egg in separate medium bowl. Pour batter into skillet; top with sausage mixture. Sprinkle with remaining ½ cup cheese.

3. Bake 20 to 25 minutes or until edges are lightly browned. Cut into wedges.

Makes 10 servings

CARAMEL APPLE SKILLET COBBLER

- 1½ cups buttermilk baking mix
- 1 cup milk
- 1 cup packed brown sugar, divided
- ½ cup sour cream
- 1 teaspoon ground cinnamon, plus additional for garnish
- ¼ cup (½ stick) butter
- ¼ teaspoon salt
- 4 Gala apples (about 1¾ pounds), peeled and cut into ¼-inch slices
- ½ cup caramel bits or unwrapped caramels cut into quarters
- Whipped cream (optional)

1. Preheat oven to 350°F.
2. Combine baking mix, milk, ½ cup brown sugar, sour cream and 1 teaspoon cinnamon in medium bowl; mix well.
3. Melt butter in large (12-inch) ovenproof skillet over medium heat. Add remaining ½ cup brown sugar and salt; cook and stir 1 minute. Add apples; stir to coat. Press apples into single layer to cover bottom of skillet; sprinkle with caramel bits. Pour batter evenly over apples.
4. Bake 40 to 45 minutes or until topping is golden brown. Cool slightly before serving. Top with whipped cream, if desired; sprinkle with additional cinnamon.

Makes 8 servings

GINGER PLUM TART

- 1 refrigerated pie crust (half of 14-ounce package)
- 1¾ pounds plums, cut into ½-inch slices
- ½ cup plus 1 teaspoon sugar, divided
- 1½ tablespoons all-purpose flour
- 1½ teaspoons ground ginger
- ¼ teaspoon ground cinnamon
- ⅛ teaspoon salt
- 1 egg
- 2 teaspoons water

1. Preheat oven to 400°F. Let pie crust stand at room temperature 10 minutes. Combine plums, ½ cup sugar, flour, ginger, cinnamon and salt in large bowl; toss to coat.
2. Roll out crust into 14-inch circle on lightly floured surface. Transfer to large (10-inch) ovenproof skillet. Mound plum mixture in center of crust, leaving 2-inch border around fruit. Fold crust up over filling, pleating as necessary and gently pressing crust into fruit to secure.
3. Beat egg and water in small bowl; brush over crust. Sprinkle with remaining 1 teaspoon sugar.*
4. Bake about 45 minutes or until crust is golden brown. Cool on wire rack. Serve warm or at room temperature.

**To add sparkle and extra crunch to the tart, use sparkling or coarse sugar to sprinkle on top instead of granulated sugar.*

Makes 6 to 8 servings

APPLE CRANBERRY CRUMBLE

- 4 large apples (about 1⅓ pounds), peeled and cut into ¼-inch slices
- 2 cups fresh or frozen cranberries
- ⅓ cup granulated sugar
- 6 tablespoons all-purpose flour, divided
- 1 teaspoon apple pie spice, divided
- ¼ teaspoon salt, divided
- ½ cup chopped walnuts
- ¼ cup old-fashioned oats
- 2 tablespoons packed brown sugar
- ¼ cup (½ stick) butter, cut into small pieces

1. Preheat oven to 375°F.
2. Combine apples, cranberries, granulated sugar, 2 tablespoons flour, ½ teaspoon apple pie spice and ⅛ teaspoon salt in large bowl; toss to coat. Spread in medium (8- to 9-inch) ovenproof skillet.
3. Combine remaining ¼ cup flour, ½ teaspoon apple pie spice, ⅛ teaspoon salt, walnuts, oats and brown sugar in medium bowl; mix well. Cut in butter with pastry blender until mixture resembles coarse crumbs. Sprinkle over fruit mixture in skillet.
4. Bake 50 to 60 minutes or until filling is bubbly and topping is lightly browned.

Makes 4 servings

WARM MIXED BERRY PIE

- 2 packages (12 ounces each) frozen mixed berries
- ⅓ cup sugar
- 3 tablespoons cornstarch
- 2 teaspoons grated orange peel
- ¼ teaspoon ground ginger
- 1 refrigerated pie crust (half of 14-ounce package)

1. Preheat oven to 350°F.
2. Combine berries, sugar, cornstarch, orange peel and ginger in large bowl; toss gently to coat. Spread in large (10-inch) ovenproof skillet.
3. Roll out crust into 12-inch circle on lightly floured surface. Place crust over fruit mixture; flute edge as desired. Cut several slits in crust to allow steam to escape.
4. Bake 1 hour or until crust is golden brown. Let stand 1 hour before serving.

Makes 8 servings

CHOCOLATE CHIP SKILLET COOKIE

- 1¾ cups all-purpose flour
- 1 teaspoon baking soda
- 1 teaspoon salt
- ¾ cup (1½ sticks) butter, softened
- ¾ cup packed brown sugar
- ½ cup granulated sugar
- 2 eggs
- 1 teaspoon vanilla
- 1 package (12 ounces) semisweet chocolate chips
- Sea salt (optional)
- Ice cream (optional)

1. Preheat oven to 350°F.
2. Combine flour, baking soda and 1 teaspoon salt in medium bowl; mix well. Beat butter, brown sugar and granulated sugar in large bowl with electric mixer at medium speed about 3 minutes or until creamy. Add eggs and vanilla; beat until well blended. Gradually add flour mixture at low speed; beat just until blended. Stir in chocolate chips.
3. Press batter evenly into well-seasoned* large (10-inch) cast iron skillet. Sprinkle lightly with sea salt, if desired.
4. Bake 35 minutes or until top and edges are golden brown but cookie is still soft in center. Cool on wire rack 10 minutes before cutting into wedges. Serve warm with ice cream, if desired.

**If skillet is not well seasoned, brush lightly with melted butter or vegetable oil. Or use large ovenproof nonstick skillet sprayed with nonstick cooking spray.*

Makes 8 servings

APPLE BERRY CINNAMON ROLL COBBLER

- 1 tablespoon cornstarch
- 2 tablespoons lemon juice
- 5 apples (about 2 pounds), peeled and cut into ½-inch pieces
- ½ cup packed brown sugar
- ¾ teaspoon ground cinnamon
- ⅛ teaspoon ground ginger
- 3 tablespoons butter
- ½ cup coarsely chopped pecans
- 1 cup fresh blueberries
- 1 package (13 ounces) refrigerated flaky cinnamon rolls with icing

1. Preheat oven to 350°F.
2. Stir cornstarch into lemon juice in small bowl until smooth. Combine apples, brown sugar, cinnamon and ginger in large bowl; mix well. Add cornstarch mixture; stir to coat.
3. Melt butter in large (12-inch) ovenproof skillet over medium heat. Add apple mixture and pecans; press into single layer to cover bottom of skillet. Sprinkle with blueberries.
4. Bake 20 minutes. Remove skillet from oven. Separate cinnamon rolls; reserve icing. Arrange cinnamon rolls over warm fruit mixture.
5. Bake 20 to 25 minutes or until filling is bubbly and cinnamon rolls are deep golden brown. Drizzle with icing. Let stand 5 minutes before serving.

Makes 8 servings

Index

Index

Index

Index

METRIC CONVERSION CHART

VOLUME MEASUREMENTS (dry)

1/8 teaspoon = 0.5 mL
1/4 teaspoon = 1 mL
1/2 teaspoon = 2 mL
3/4 teaspoon = 4 mL
1 teaspoon = 5 mL
1 tablespoon = 15 mL
2 tablespoons = 30 mL
1/4 cup = 60 mL
1/3 cup = 75 mL
1/2 cup = 125 mL
2/3 cup = 150 mL
3/4 cup = 175 mL
1 cup = 250 mL
2 cups = 1 pint = 500 mL
3 cups = 750 mL
4 cups = 1 quart = 1 L

VOLUME MEASUREMENTS (fluid)

1 fluid ounce (2 tablespoons) = 30 mL
4 fluid ounces (1/2 cup) = 125 mL
8 fluid ounces (1 cup) = 250 mL
12 fluid ounces (1 1/2 cups) = 375 mL
16 fluid ounces (2 cups) = 500 mL

WEIGHTS (mass)

1/2 ounce = 15 g
1 ounce = 30 g
3 ounces = 90 g
4 ounces = 120 g
8 ounces = 225 g
10 ounces = 285 g
12 ounces = 360 g
16 ounces = 1 pound = 450 g

DIMENSIONS

1/16 inch = 2 mm
1/8 inch = 3 mm
1/4 inch = 6 mm
1/2 inch = 1.5 cm
3/4 inch = 2 cm
1 inch = 2.5 cm

OVEN TEMPERATURES

250°F = 120°C
275°F = 140°C
300°F = 150°C
325°F = 160°C
350°F = 180°C
375°F = 190°C
400°F = 200°C
425°F = 220°C
450°F = 230°C

BAKING PAN SIZES

Utensil	Size in Inches/Quarts	Metric Volume	Size in Centimeters
Baking or Cake Pan (square or rectangular)	8×8×2	2 L	20×20×5
	9×9×2	2.5 L	23×23×5
	12×8×2	3 L	30×20×5
	13×9×2	3.5 L	33×23×5
Loaf Pan	8×4×3	1.5 L	20×10×7
	9×5×3	2 L	23×13×7
Round Layer Cake Pan	8×1½	1.2 L	20×4
	9×1½	1.5 L	23×4
Pie Plate	8×1¼	750 mL	20×3
	9×1¼	1 L	23×3
Baking Dish or Casserole	1 quart	1 L	—
	1½ quart	1.5 L	—
	2 quart	2 L	—